Cancer Changes Everything

By
Pam Pottorff

This book is dedicated to
my sister Barb, The Warrior Chick

*"If life is to have meaning and if God's will
is to be done,
all of us have to accept who we are and
what we are,
give it back to God, and thank Him for the
way He made us.
What I am is God's gift to me.
What I do with it is my gift to Him."*
                              -Warren W. Wiersbe

Chapter 1
That's How the Cookie
Crumbles

Ah, Billy Joel's Greatest Hits. I removed the disk from the CD holder attached to the visor on the passenger side of my car. I kissed the CD knowing that would be the closest I would ever come to kissing Billy Joel then I quickly popped the disk into the player. I cranked the volume, and slowly backed out of the garage. As I cruised down the highway, the car windows vibrated with the rhythm of the bass as I sang along to "Piano Man," "The Entertainer," and "A New York State of Mind."

Once I had entered the city limits of Colorado Springs, I decreased my speed and rolled down the windows enjoying the fresh air. Before I knew it, I was at an intersection waiting for the traffic light to change from red to green. I continued to sing and rock out to the song "Moving Out." The driver in the car next to mine was staring in disbelief so I gave him the twinkling finger wave and a smile as I continued to bounce along with the beat of the music. Fortunately for both of us, the light changed, and I continued on my journey.

It was a gorgeous July morning with a cloudless sky. Because I was a teacher, during the summer breaks I always took my kids for their annual medical and dental check-ups. Today it was my turn. I was on my way to have a mammogram. My children, Landon who was eleven and fifteen year old Sierra, were still asleep in their beds when I left the house. For this appointment, I was going solo.

In a matter of minutes I was at the medical clinic, parking my car, and entering the building. Billy Joel would have to wait.

I checked in and completed the procedure in a matter of minutes. I was waiting in the holding area still wearing my stylish, threadbare, hospital gown, when the technician suddenly appeared before me.

"The doctor wants a closer look at an area in your right breast. He would like you to have an ultrasound to gather more information," she explained.

"When?"

"Now."

This cannot be good, I thought to myself as she led me to another waiting room. I sat down and began to flip through the pages of a magazine, gazing at the photographs because I was too nervous to read the text.

Another technician appeared at the door. She instructed me to follow her through a maze of hallways to a chilly, dark room about the size of a large walk-in closet. The ultrasound equipment took up the entire room except for a small area occupied by the technician's chair. The procedure was finished in twenty minutes.

"Just stay here in case the doctor needs additional images," the technician informed me in a monotone voice. Then she left me alone in the cold, dark cave.

By now my nervous energy had turned into outright fear. I began to shiver. I couldn't tell if the shivering was from being frightened or the chilly temperature of the room. At this point in my life, my father had battled lung and prostate cancer. My brother had died of colon cancer, and my sister had fought melanoma for many years. I had seen first-hand what they had gone through, and I was scared the same might happen to me. My mind kept playing possible scenarios over and over in my head, and none of them were positive. I knew I needed to stop these negative thoughts so I tried to sing "Piano Man," but I couldn't remember the words. *Are you kidding me?* I had been singing this song since high school. I had it memorized, but at that moment in time, I felt like all the contents of my brain had been wiped out and replaced by fear.

I had been sitting shivering on the edge of the examination table for an extremely long time. In an effort to warm myself and calm my fears, I jumped down from the table and began walking around the ultrasound machine.

A knock on the door startled me, and I quickly jumped back on the table as if I had never left my spot. I folded my hands on my lap hoping to create the illusion that I was calm and confident even though I was feeling the exact opposite. The technician had returned along with an older gentleman. When he approached, I could see his nametag indicated he was a doctor. *This cannot be good,* a little voice in my head whispered.

Over the years I had experienced many mammograms. The technicians always left me in the waiting room while a doctor somewhere in the building looked at the images. The illusive doctor always reminded me of the great and powerful Oz in the movie "The Wizard of Oz." He or she was

6

the all-knowing and all-powerful being who seemed to hold my future in their hands at that moment, yet I had never seen this person. I must admit there were times over the years that I wondered if the mammogram-reading physician even existed. So when this mythical doctor appeared in the flesh, shook my hand, and introduced himself, I knew I was in trouble . . . big trouble.

"As you know we have been monitoring a suspicious spot on your right breast for several years," the doctor explained as he sat in the chair beside the exam table. "The mammogram indicated the area in question has changed, and the ultrasound confirms it. Because of that change, I want you to have a needle biopsy. It is a painless procedure in which a needle will be inserted into the area in question and a few cells will be extracted to see if they are malignant."

In my realm of thinking malignant translates into the word cancer. Both words describe mutated, rogue cells that can reproduce and eventually kill a person. My analogy of the situation was a civil war raging in your own body with the good, healthy cells battling the evil, mutated cells. While this was what I was thinking on the inside, I managed to remain calm on the outside as the doctor continued to explain the needle biopsy. I tried desperately to concentrate on what he was saying. I knew his lips were moving, but after he said the word malignant, all I heard was "blah, blah, blah." I came back to reality when he handed me a slip of paper and asked me to make an appointment for the needle biopsy at the front desk.

"The earliest appointment we have for that procedure is one week from today on July 18th," the receptionist said as she looked up from her computer.

"That date and time will be fine," I responded as the receptionist filled out a card to remind me of the appointment. Then she handed me the reminder card and a sheet of paper containing instructions I would need to follow before the procedure. When I reached my car, I sat in the driver's seat for a few minutes to calm myself and process the events that had just occurred. Finally, I turned the key in the ignition and was greeted by Billy Joel belting out "Only the Good Die Young." I quickly turned off the blaring sound system.

Not now, Billy. Not now. Not that song. I laid my head on the steering wheel in an effort to compose myself for the trip home. Unlike my lively drive to the medical center that morning, I now drove home in complete silence. Visions of my dad, brother, and sister, all who had been diagnosed with cancer, flashed through my head.

Dad's Herculean body had never spent a day in a gym. He worked out daily, from sunrise to sunset, on our Iowa farm. He was in excellent physical health until he had a cancer-riddled lung removed. Suddenly, the man who had thrown hundreds of hay bales and mucked out the barn countless times, could no longer walk across a room without becoming weak and breathless.

I thought of my brother Steve. He was ten years my senior so to me he was Superman in every sense of the word. Although Superman had superhuman powers in the movies, he had something that deprived him of his strength. That something was kryptonite. Steve was no different. His kryptonite was colon cancer. Although he fought the dreaded disease for several years with stamina, humor, dignity, and grace, it eventually took his life. When his condition was classified as terminal, I flew from my home in Colorado back to Iowa to spend a week with Steve. It was a week filled with memories, laughter, and sorrow. We both knew it would be the last time I would hear Steve's voice, see the mischievous twinkle in his eyes, and enjoy his cheesy grin. When I hugged him for one last time, cancer had reduced the once healthy, vibrant body of "my Superman" to mere skin stretched over bones.

My sister Barb had battled melanoma for such a long period of time that I could no longer keep track of the years. She was my "warrior chick," who battled with every ounce of her being, with every skill and weapon she had in her arsenal, yet through it all she remained a vision of loveliness with her hair styled and her nails polished. Her greatest weapon was her uncanny sense of humor. After one of her many surgeries to remove sections of her malignant flesh, she reported to me that the area involved was her derriere. "Now I can truthfully say that cancer is a real pain in the butt," she told me. We both laughed, and yet we both realized cancer is anything but funny.

As these visions flashed in my imagination, I wondered if I was about to embark on a similar journey as these three people. Granted, I had been a bystander in their circumstances, but that was no easy role. Watching someone you care about suffer, knowing there is nothing you can do about the situation, was at the very least a cruel form of torture.

Fortunately, these visions stopped when I reached our house. The kids were up, dressed, and had just finished lunch. Landon was off to hang out with a friend, and Sierra was headed back to her room. My husband, a middle school assistant principal, was at work interviewing teacher candidates for the upcoming school year. Basically I was by myself, and it was time to decompress.

People deal with stress in a variety of ways. Some people find a glass of wine, exercise, or music to be helpful. Unusual as it may sound, my go to stress relief strategy was to eat raw chocolate chip cookie dough. There is something self indulgent about the act of eating raw cookie dough. Because it is raw, it has an element of danger about it. Its creamy texture and the explosion of flavor when I bit into a chocolate chip made me feel I was worth every calorie.

I found my favorite recipe and began making the delicious delicacy. When the dough was complete, I began dropping blobs of it onto the cookie sheets. The process reminded me of a game we used to play as kids. We would pluck petals off a flower one at a time saying the words, "He loves me. He loves me not." Whatever you said as the last petal was picked told you if a boy liked you or not. Truly scientific, I know. As I plopped a mound of cookie dough onto the sheet, I said the

10

words, "I do have cancer." Then I popped a ball of dough into my mouth saying the words, "I don't have cancer." I repeated the sequence with every glob of dough, being careful to end each sequence by popping a blob into my mouth and saying the words, "I don't have cancer," with the hope that this superstitious activity would determine my diagnosis . . . my future. That evening after dinner I placed a small plate of cookies on the table for dessert.

"That's all the cookies there are? I thought you made a whole batch," my daughter inquired. "What happened to the rest?"

"I ate them," I cheerfully confessed.

"You mean you ate the dough?"

"Yep," I said with a sense of pride.

"Mom, you shouldn't be doing that. Cookie dough has raw eggs in it. It's not good for you," she scolded.

"Well, Sylvester Stallone ate raw eggs in the movie 'Rocky' and look what it did for him," I responded.

She grabbed a cookie from the plate and gave me the teenage eye roll. If she only knew what kind of day I had experienced, she would have encouraged me to eat cookie dough and a few other decadent foods. How ironic she thought cookie dough was bad for my health. That's nothing compared to having cancer.

When we went to bed that evening, I told my husband Greg about the events of the day. He sweetly kissed my forehead, held me close, and told me everything was going to be all right. At that moment in time, I believed him.

11

The next week actually flew by. Fortunately, when I arrived at the medical clinic for the needle biopsy, I didn't have to wait long. I was relieved because waiting allows negative thoughts to creep into my otherwise positive mind.

It was obvious the woman who performed the procedure had completed hundreds, if not thousands, of needle biopsies. She informed me I could watch what was happening inside my body on a large screen, which was mounted on the wall in front of me. She warned me that many people were too squeamish to observe the procedure on the screen. Not me, I assured her. I thought it was fascinating. I appreciated how she meticulously explained every step before completing it. There was a small pinch then I watched the needle enter my body. The biopsy was quick and painless. The final step was to insert a marker to make it easier to find the area in question again. The collected cells would be sent to a lab, and it would be several weeks before there would be results. This would be one more lesson in patience.

Fast forward to a Friday afternoon in early August. School had started for the year and a fresh group of eager third graders had become my new class, my new family. The students had been dismissed for the day and were on their way home to spend time with their families for the weekend. I was preparing my classroom and teaching materials for the coming week when my cell phone rang. It was my primary care physician. Due to his busy schedule and my inability to answer the phone while I was teaching during the day, he usually called me with test results in the evenings, so a phone call from him in the afternoon was quite unusual.

"I have the results of your needle biopsy," he began the conversation. Then he paused. "The cells are malignant."

I didn't respond. I was shocked to be told such life-changing information over the phone. I had assumed when a doctor shared a cancer diagnosis with you, it would be done in a face-to-face meeting.

"Pam, are you still there?"

"Yeah, I'm still here. What do I need to do next?"

"We are going to set you up with the best breast specialist in the region. I've already completed the referral so all systems are go in terms of your health insurance. All you need to do is call her office and set up an appointment," he continued then he gave me her phone number. He assured me that finding the cancer cells so early was definitely going to benefit me.

"Don't worry. We are going to take good care of you," he continued in a calm reassuring voice.

"Thank you. You always have taken good care of me, and I don't expect this situation to be any different. I appreciate you and all you have done for me," I shared. I ended the call and finished preparing my classroom.

Our son Landon went to school with me each day. He usually spent time after school with the other teachers' kids in the computer lab playing games while I worked in my classroom. I rounded up Landon, telling him it was time to head home. Usually we had a nice conversation in the car about how his day went, but on this day we drove home in silence.

I shared the information with my husband that evening but not with my children. I thought it would be best to wait until I was further along in the process before I told them.

Before falling asleep that night I had decided I wasn't going to lament the fact I had cancer. I wasn't going to take part in any form of self-pity or ask the haunting, unanswerable question, "Why me?" What good would any of that do? We don't know why certain things happen to us in our lives. It's all just part of God's plan, and that's how the cookie crumbles.

Greg, Landon, Sierra, and Pam

14

Chapter 2
The "C" Word

Even though the next day was Saturday, a day I normally slept in, I woke up early because I was attending the Women of Faith Conference in Denver with a group of friends from work. For this annual pilgrimage, we always met in the parking lot of a local grocery store where we would leave our cars and pile into our friend's gigantic vehicle. As we neared the Pepsi Center where the conference was held, the conversation went from expressing our challenges and concerns about work to all the things we were thankful for.

"At least we can be thankful you don't have cancer," one friend expressed as she glanced my way. I had told this group about my mammogram, ultra sound, and biopsy. I think because the entire process had taken so long, they assumed I had received a clean bill of health.

"Actually, I do have cancer," I shared. "My doctor called yesterday after school to tell me."

There was a fleeting moment of silence as my news soaked into their heads and hearts. Silence was something that rarely occurred when we were together. We were constantly talking and laughing. It was just who we were as a group.

Finally, the driver broke the silence. " I'm sorry to hear that. You're going to be okay. Doctors know so much more about cancer than they did in the past."

"I am going to be okay," I said with so much confidence that I shocked myself. "Whatever the doctors tell me to do, I'm going to do it."

"A positive attitude can be the best medicine," someone added.

"We will all pray for you," another friend offered.

"I appreciate that. I'll take all the prayers I can get. Today is my first full day of living with the news that I have cancer, and there are no other people I would rather be with and nothing else I would rather be doing than experiencing this conference with all of you," I shared. That last statement was so true. Sharing the day with such good friends made me feel positive and peaceful. It was so much better than being at home wallowing in self-pity, and I was determined not to do that.

Throughout the conference I felt God's loving presence, which often physically manifested itself in the form of goose bumps. The inspirational speakers ignited my spirit and rekindled my faith, reminding me God had always taken good care of me, and this situation would be no different. Singing along with the musical groups gave me emotional strength and courage.

Whenever there was a break at the conference, my friends would shuffle our seating arrangement so that I was always sitting by someone different. They showed their support with simple meaningful actions such as touching my arm, rubbing my back, or flashing me a smile. One friend just sat down beside me, put her head on my shoulder and sighed. Although few words were spoken that day, I received their messages loud and clear. With a friendship like ours, words weren't necessary. I knew they had my back. I knew they loved me and would be there to help and support me through every step of this uncertain journey I was about to embark upon. In our hearts we believed the challenge I was about to face was only going to make our friendship grow in depth.

After the conference ended, the conversation in the car on the way back to the grocery store parking lot centered on a wrap up of the inspiration we had received and how we could use our newfound positive energy in our daily lives. Outside of the grocery store we completed our ritual of hugging good-bye before we each got into our cars to drive to our homes. I must admit the hugs on this particular evening lasted a little longer, were a little sweeter, and definitely had more meaning.

Women of Faith Conference

As I drove home in silence that night, the events of the day replayed in my head like a series of video clips. Nationally known speakers and musicians had inspired me. I had felt the love and support of my dear friends. I had felt the presence of God and the peace in knowing He would always care for me. Ironically, for it being my first full twenty-four hours living with a cancer diagnosis, it was a pretty awesome day. It could have easily been a day with an impending cloud of doom hanging over my head, but instead the day was truly a refreshing, unexpected gift.

As I drove home that evening the words of the world famous philosopher, Forest Gump echoed in my head. "Life is like a box of chocolates. You never know what you are going to get." A more accurate analogy for me has always been that life is a rollercoaster filled with a series of ups and downs. Just as on a rollercoaster, in life when you experience the down part of the ride, you can see the hill, the upside, just ahead of you. There is an exciting anticipation that is a strange mixture of fear and exhilaration. Once you reach the summit of a rollercoaster, the view is spectacular. You briefly experience a twisted sense of accomplishment, before crashing to the basin ahead of you, reaching the bottom only to climb the next incline and have the entire process start all over again.

It was at that moment, alone in my car, I realized the rollercoaster ride of cancer diagnosis was going to include many ups and downs, but I was determined when I experienced the down parts I was going to look ahead to the climb, to the summit, to the up side that was just ahead of me if I would only open my eyes and look.

The following day was Sunday so I headed to church with my family. The music at Sunday service was so intense and beautiful, and the sermon seemed to have been written just for me. I focused my prayers on thanking God for all the blessings He had bestowed on me rather than dwelling on the challenges that were looming in my near future.

Later that afternoon, I called my friend Ginger, who had been the art teacher at our school before she retired. Just a few years earlier she had been diagnosed with breast cancer. I thought perhaps she could give me some helpful hints as well as some much-needed encouragement. She came through with flying colors on both accounts just like I knew she would.

Shortly after our phone conversation ended, I began to remember how Ginger had shared the news of her diagnosis with all of us. It was at our weekly morning staff meeting. Ginger shared the news of her diagnosis and went on to explain in detail the steps of her treatment plan including surgery, chemotherapy, and radiation. At first we were all shocked by this unexpected news. When reality finally set in, the tears flowed freely in the room. Suddenly the bell rang, and the students flooded into the hallways and eventually the classrooms. I know we were all thinking the same thing. How were we going to face the kids with our puffy, tear-filled eyes, and even worse, our burdened hearts?

Ginger stood by the door, and we each hugged her as we exited the library to journey to our classrooms. Leaving the library felt like leaving a funeral, which was crazy because Ginger wasn't dead. Were we getting ahead of ourselves? Just because a person has been diagnosed with cancer doesn't mean that person is going to die. People do survive this disease. Ginger was still full of life, still her colorful, flamboyant, lively self. We should have been celebrating her life, her strength, her very being rather than mourning her diagnosis.

My friends who I had shared my diagnosis with during the conference over the weekend were also my coworkers. I couldn't expect them to keep my news a secret. That was too much to ask, so I knew I needed to develop a plan to tell the staff, the parent community, and my beloved students.

That Sunday afternoon I sat at my computer and composed an email to the staff. I decided to take what I called "the Mary Poppins' approach." Just like the song from the movie suggested, "just a spoonful of sugar makes the medicine go down," I thought a healthy dose of humor could make my situation a bit more palatable. So I added a little comic relief in the subject line of the email.

To: The Larkspur Elementary Staff
Subject: Keeping you abreast of a situation

Dear Friends,

My doctor called me Friday afternoon to tell me that I have breast cancer. Through mammograms and ultrasounds over several years, doctors have monitored the area in question closely, and therefore the cancer was caught at the earliest stage possible. I will undergo surgery, but the verdict is still out about my post surgery treatment plan.

I talked to my sister over the weekend. She has bravely battled skin cancer for over twelve years. She gave me these wonderful words of wisdom, "You may have cancer, but cancer doesn't have you." Life goes on and so will I. My plan is a simple one. I will do whatever my team of doctors tells me to do, and I will keep my attitude positive. Simple. That's how I like it.

I hope this situation doesn't make you feel uncomfortable. I am still the same quirky Pam who loves you with all my heart. I am thanking you in advance for your prayers and support as I travel through this challenging journey.

Love,
Pam

I read the message several times, continually changing the text to communicate the necessary information in a positive manner. When I finally completed the task, I sat for a moment staring at the computer screen in disbelief. Somehow seeing my situation in writing made it seem very real. I took a deep breath. As I let it out, I pressed the send button knowing at that instant my "secret" would be shared with the entire staff. Soon it would be the hot topic of many conversations in the teachers' lounge. I felt confident and positive about the way I had chosen to share this information. Sending the email Sunday night meant many people would read the news that evening or Monday morning before school began. The first sentence said it all, and each person could decide to continue to read the message or stop to read it at a more convenient time. Truly, that was my goal, to give my friends and coworkers time. Time to process the situation. Time to collect their thoughts and decide how they were going to react. The last thing I wanted to do was to force someone into an uncomfortable situation.

I felt like I was on a roll, so I moved on to the next task, which was to secure a substitute teacher to take over my class throughout my treatment. I knew just the person to be my better half in this situation . . . my friend, Joy. Her name says it all. She did bring so much joy to everyone she ever interacted with. Joy had been a reading specialist at our school until her position was cut due to budget issues. She had worked miracles with my son, Landon, so I knew her skills were extraordinary. After her job was cut, she had substituted in all of our classrooms. I loved how she completed everything I ever asked her to do. I loved how she interacted with the kids. Plain and simple, she loved the students, and they loved her right back.

That's not something you learn in a college course or at a teacher in-service. You either have it or you don't. It's in your gut, and your very soul. Fortunately, Joy had it in spades. I called Joy and explained my situation to her.

I ended the conversation with, "Will you help me? Are you in?"

"I'm in!" she exclaimed. Those words lifted a great burden from my mind because I knew my students would be with the best possible teacher I could secure for them. Joy had always been a trusted coworker, as well as a dear, sweet friend, and little did I know it, but in the coming weeks she actually would become a heroine to the kids and to me.

With the best possible substitute teacher in the world in my back pocket, I felt up to the challenge of breaking the news of my cancer diagnosis to my students' parents. Once again, I sat at my laptop staring at the blank screen. Even though every Sunday evening I sent an email to the parents outlining our learning and homework for the week, I knew this Sunday's email was going to be anything but routine. It was going to be a bombshell.

I felt the best strategy would be to ease into the news. I explained what we would be learning, homework, and projects for the week. No problem. Now it was time for the revelation.

"On a personal note, through a series of recent tests and procedures, I have been diagnosed with breast cancer." There, I had done it. I had written the "C word." I went on to briefly explain my possible treatment options. I was very careful to explain I had retained Joy as my substitute teacher for every day I would be out of the classroom. I explained the stability of having the same guest teacher, who already knew the students, and was clearly over qualified for the job. I wanted to communicate to the parents that the education of their children was of the utmost importance to me. Finally, I ended with asking the parents not to tell their children about my diagnosis. I wanted to do that myself first thing on Monday morning. I knew in my heart the parents would respect my wishes.

Finally, I composed an email to the school principal, summarizing my situation, explaining my plan of having Joy as my substitute throughout my journey, my communication with the parents, and my plan of sharing with the students on Monday morning. I wanted him to know the situation was under control, which is something cancer patients desperately search for . . . control.

By now it was 1 a.m., and I was physically and emotionally exhausted. I dragged myself into the bedroom, and put on my pajamas. Too exhausted to brush my teeth, I flopped into the bed eager for sleep to overtake my overactive mind, but it was difficult. I still hadn't decided how I was going to tell my students. Images of me frozen speechless in front of the class continually ran through my imagination until exhaustion replaced those images with slumber. Tomorrow was another day. I knew God would help me find the right way to talk to the kids. He would give me the words and the empathy for the challenge.

Monday morning arrived faster than I had anticipated. I was always one of the first people to arrive at school each morning so as usual no one was there yet. This was fortunate because I had time to flip on my computer and read several emails from coworkers and parents expressing their empathy regarding my situation. As the morning progressed a few staff members trickled into my classroom to offer their love and support. I felt calm until the time for the bell to ring drew near. My stomach suddenly was in knots, and my palms started to sweat. I tried to convince myself that it was just another Monday morning, but in my heart I knew that wasn't true.

I situated myself outside the classroom door like I did every day. I always greeted my students with hugs, high fives, or fist bumps, whatever felt most comfortable for each individual. Former students always stopped by on the way to their classrooms to receive hugs or a few words of encouragement. Soon the second bell rang. The students were at their desks completing their morning work while I completed lunch count and attendance on the computer. It did seem like an average Monday morning until I asked the students to sit in a big circle on the floor. We only did this for class meetings or for a weekly book discussion we called Socratic Seminar. It was at this point they knew something was up.

"I've got some good news and some bad news," I started the conversation. "What do you want to hear first, the good or the bad?"

"The bad," they chimed in unison. I knew it. This goofy group would always choose to start with the bad news.

"During the next few weeks and months I will need to miss a few days of school for several doctor's appointments. But here is the good news. Every time I am gone Mrs. Joy Wagner will be your substitute teacher. That's good news, right? You all know her, and she is so good to you," I continued. I could see by their facial expressions that the wheels were turning inside of their heads and soon the barge of questions would begin.

"Are you sick, Mrs. Pottorff?" a student asked.

Hmmmmm. I hadn't thought of myself as being sick. I wasn't sure how to answer this question so it was at this point I let God take over and do the talking.

"I'm not really sick," I explained. "My body isn't working correctly right now. It's malfunctioning. Let me explain it to you. First, I just want you to sit silently for thirty seconds. Can you do that?"

Yes. They all agreed they could complete that task. In fact, thinking in silence was a skill we had been working on. We called it "think time." Its purpose was to allow them time to think about what had just been said as well as to give them time to organize their thoughts before verbalizing them.

When the thirty seconds was up I asked them what they thought was happening inside their bodies during that time. Of course, several students responded that their hearts were beating. Their lungs were breathing, and blood was traveling all

26

over their bodies. I told them all of their answers were correct, and several of them beamed with pride.

"What was also happening was your bodies were busy making cells," I added. We had briefly studied cells as the building blocks of our bodies so they were familiar with the concept. "Isn't it amazing that your body makes cells without you telling it to? It's automatic and just happens. You can't even feel it. Your bodies make lots of cells every day because you are kids, and you are growing. Do you think I am still growing and making cells?"

"Of course, you're not growing. You're a grown-up! " a brave student chuckled seeing humor in the situation.

"You're right. I'm not growing any more, thank goodness, otherwise I would be huge," I added as the class laughed at the idea. "But does my body still make cells?"

They didn't have an answer to that question so I continued, " Our cells work so hard that they wear out and die so our bodies are always making new cells to replace the worn out ones. Your bodies create extra cells because you are growing. My body only makes replacement cells. Does that make sense?"

They all nodded their heads in agreement.

"My body has been making some cells that are not formed correctly. It is like your body is a cell factory, and sometimes factories make things that have defects or imperfections. I need to have these abnormal cells taken out of my body before they

27

create more abnormal cells. When your body starts making abnormal cells, it is commonly referred to as having cancer. How many of you know someone who has had cancer?"

I knew all of their hands would go up because they all knew Ginger Hodges, our former art teacher who had battled breast cancer. But I also knew every child in our classroom knew someone else with the disease, and I wanted to give them the opportunity to share their experiences.

I was very glad I did. Every child shared a story about an aunt, uncle, grandparent, neighbor, or friend who had been diagnosed with cancer. This discussion seemed to be very therapeutic for the kids. They shared that often they didn't feel comfortable talking about cancer because it was a sad and frightening thing to discuss. One student explained she felt if she talked about her grandfather having cancer it meant he would die. It was as if it were a superstition. As long as she didn't talk about it, he would stay alive. Fortunately, her family had helped her realize her belief wasn't true, and they could talk about the situation as a family. Her honest confession led me to the following statement.

"I don't want any of you to be sad or frightened about my condition. I will be totally honest with you about what is happening. I will answer any questions you may have," I shared.

"I do have a question, Mrs. Pottorff. What is going to happen to you?" a student asked.

"I am going to have surgery to take out the unhealthy cells."

"Will your hair fall out like Mrs. Hodges?"

"If some of the abnormal cells have traveled to other parts of my body, I will have chemotherapy. During chemotherapy chemicals are put in your body to kill the cancer cells. Unfortunately, those chemicals kill the unhealthy cells and some of the healthy cells as well. That's why Mrs. Hodges' hair fell out, and she was sick during her treatments. Her good and her bad cells were being destroyed. If the abnormal cells are just in one spot then I will have radiation treatments, which will kill the cancer cells just on that particular area of my body. I won't lose my hair or be sick, but I may feel tired."

The students seemed satisfied by my answers, and even comforted by my honesty. I believe the comfort level and positive atmosphere lead to the question every one of them was thinking but was afraid to ask. It was inevitable, and finally one student mustered up enough courage to ask.

"Mrs. Pottorff, are you going to die?"

I knew that question was going to come up in the conversation, but I was still unprepared to answer it. It was time once again to let God take over.

"Let's face it. We are all going to die sooner or later. No one lives forever. I think you are no longer little kids, and you can understand that idea. You are kids who can handle thinking about tough topics like this. That is part of growing up," I began. "I don't know when I will die, but I will tell you what I do know. I know the unhealthy cells in my body were discovered very early. I know I will do whatever my doctors tell me to do. Because of

29

those two factors, I know I am not going to die of cancer right now."

I so desperately wanted the students to believe that last sentence even though I was unsure if I believed it myself. I did believe the fact the cancer was discovered at such an early stage, and my willingness to cooperate and maintain a positive outlook were huge favorable factors. On the flip side, I had watched my brother die of the disease. I knew doctors could cut the mutated cells out of your body. The cells could be killed with chemicals and radiation. Unfortunately, when the cancer reoccurs, it comes back with a vengeance even stronger than before. That thought was my greatest fear, but I refused to let the kids see that fear. I didn't want to scare them. There was no point in that. I had decided my transparency and honesty with them had a limit, and we had reached it.

I think the students realized we had reached the end of our conversation as well. One brave soul stood up from her spot in the circle, walked towards me, and gave me a big bear hug. Soon a line formed in front of me with each student waiting patiently to give me a hug filled with encouragement and understanding. Even the boys in the class, who preferred high fives or fist bumps, hugged me that day. It was a moment in time I will always cherish.

We returned to our daily routine, and everything seemed to be back to normal. Lunchtime rolled around rather quickly. I walked the students to the cafeteria but decided to walk past the teachers' lounge and not go in. I had spent the majority of the morning in a deep conversation with the students about my situation. I wasn't up to a similar conversation in the lounge with my peers. It was a good decision. I used the time to call the breast specialist's office to set up an appointment. Then I called Joy to see if she could cover the afternoon of the appointment, and I completed the necessary steps in the district's sub system to make sure Joy was my sub for that day. Since we didn't live in the school district in which I taught, Landon was open enrolled. So my final task was to call the transportation department to arrange for Landon to be dropped off at a bus stop about fifteen minutes from our home.

To be honest, I was tired of waiting for tests and test results. I wanted this journey to begin so that I would be closer to it ending. That afternoon I started the wheels in motion, knowing full well once the process began I couldn't stop it.

Larkspur Elementary School

Chapter 3
The Luck of the Draw

When I opened the door of the renowned breast specialist's office, I thought I had entered someone's living room. I took a step back through the doorway to peer at the office number and name plaque in the hall in order to make sure I was in the right place. The waiting area was small and cozy, filled with casual, comfortable furniture. Lamps strategically placed throughout the room gave the environment a warm, inviting glow. No one was at the front desk so I snuggled into the cushions of the couch.

In a matter of minutes, the perky receptionist showed up at the desk.

"You must be Pam. I have you all checked in. Just follow me."

I'm going to like this place, I thought to myself.

Once we entered the examination room, the perky receptionist transformed into a warm-hearted nurse who took my blood pressure, height, weight, and temperature then left me with a hospital gown to wear.

Minutes later there was a knock on the door, and the doctor entered the room. She was a friendly, middle-aged woman who wore casual clothing and very little makeup. Her easy-going demeanor immediately put me at ease. She asked me a few questions as she glanced through my file, finally focusing on the images of my right breast. Silence. I could tell she was thinking, probably contemplating my future so I was quiet.

"Let's take a look," she said as she carefully opened the gown. " Oh my, these are going to have to go."

To tell the truth I was shocked by her statement, thinking she was suggesting a mastectomy. I didn't think my case was that complicated or drastic. "What do you mean?" I asked.

"Has anyone ever suggested breast reduction to you?" she continued.

"No. I thought that would be a cosmetic surgery, which wouldn't be covered by insurance. I could never afford anything like that," I explained.

"There are medical reasons to have breast reduction surgery, which means insurance would cover it. Doesn't your back hurt?" she asked.

"It's not my back that hurts. It's my shoulders." I moved the gown from my shoulders to reveal two deep, red, irritated indentations from my bra straps.

"We can take care of that for you," the doctor began. "We can do a breast reduction surgery. We will take out the malignant cells along with a lot of your breast tissue, which should alleviate your shoulder and back pain. What do you think?"

I was speechless. My breasts had been extremely large since I was in high school. I had always tried to hide them by walking slumped over and wearing baggy clothing. My large breasts made physical activities like running or jumping very painful. Having smaller breasts would be a dream come true. I couldn't believe that a negative, such as being diagnosed with breast cancer, could have such a positive outcome. It was the up side of life's roller coaster.

"I love this idea," I responded. "It's a win/win situation!"

"It truly is," the doctor added. "Another bonus to this procedure is that because you have so much excess breast tissue which we can remove, we won't need to worry about the margins around the malignant area. If you agree this is the path we should take, I would like to explain the procedure to you."

"I definitely think this is what we should do. I agree one hundred percent," I assured her.

"I usually do this surgery with a plastic surgeon. There are two I like to work with. One is new to the area. He is young, but he has a great reputation for knowing what is current in his field. The other doctor is a veteran physician with many years of experience. Both men are excellent at what they do. You can't go wrong with either choice," she explained.

Even though I dreaded any kind of surgery, I felt my fear and apprehension slowly melting away with every word she spoke.

"Basically we are going to take your breasts apart, remove the excess tissue including the cancer cells, then put your breasts back together," she explained as she showed me on my body where the incisions would be located.

"Sounds good! Let's do it! What do I need to do next?" I asked.

"Pick a plastic surgeon and set up an appointment with him," she answered.

I felt the breast specialist's experience and intelligence were going to offer me the opportunity to change my life for the better. Her calm, reassuring demeanor and her exquisite idea regarding the breast reduction surgery touched my heart. I asked her if I could give her a hug as a symbol of my appreciation and gratitude.

After she left the room, I dressed and headed to the waiting room to checkout. Of course, the nurse had transformed back into the receptionist.

"Have you decided which plastic surgeon you would like to work with?" she asked.

I chose the younger doctor simply because the specialist had mentioned him first. It was the luck of the draw as my dad used to say.

"Let's give his office a call right now and get an appointment scheduled for you," the receptionist told me.

I was impressed by her willingness to make the phone call and get the ball rolling. I had assumed it would be my responsibility to make the call. She picked up the phone and in a matter of minutes I had an appointment scheduled with the plastic surgeon for the following week.

"I'll fax today's report to the plastic surgeon's office right away," the receptionist informed me.

As I made my way to the parking lot, I thought how today's events were another example of what I had begun to call "the up side of down." It was based on my idea that life is a series of ups and downs just like a roller coaster ride. Just like when you are on the down part of a roller coaster, you can see the up side just ahead, I was committed to looking for the upside of every down situation life had to throw at me.

I had arrived at the specialist's office expecting her to tell me I was either going to have a lumpectomy or a mastectomy. Either way, I knew there was going to be an "ectomy" involved. Never in my wildest dreams could I have ever imagined I could have breast reduction surgery, which would remove the cancer cells as well as improve my health by reducing my breast size. This was the best possible scenario. It truly was the up side of down, a blessing in disguise.

One week later when I entered the office of the plastic surgeon, I noticed how it was the complete opposite of the specialist's warm and cozy environment. Many sections of the building the office was located in weren't even completed yet.

The overhead fluorescent lights glared off the chrome frames of the contemporary furniture. Glass tables strewn with magazines completed the sleek, modern look of the space. I checked in with one of the many people behind the front desk then parked myself on one of the black leather sofas to enjoy reading a novel I had stuffed into my purse.

Soon I was in an exam room putting on a plush terry cloth robe, which was quite a contrast to the thin, cotton, hospital gown I was accustomed to. Obviously, the clientele here was a little different.

The young doctor entered the room, performed an exam, and explained the surgery to me. Eager to move the process forward, I assured him I understood the procedure and asked him what I needed to do next. He told me a nurse would give me a packet of instructions to follow before the surgery. On my way out I needed to schedule the surgery with someone at the front desk. His staff would take care of all the details including contacting the breast specialist so she could assist him with the procedure.

When I returned home that afternoon, I immediately called Joy to tell her the date of the surgery would be Tuesday, September 27th. I would take Tuesday, Wednesday, Thursday and Friday off from work to recover. Those days would be followed by a weekend, and I would be able to return to work on Monday morning. Joy voiced her concern about such a short recovery time. Honestly, I had thought the same thing myself, but the plastic surgeon had assured me I would be able to return to work on Monday morning. Secretly, in the back of my mind, I wondered if he knew how much energy it took to teach twenty-seven third graders every day. He only dealt with one patient at a time, and they were adults.

I forged on with the next task, which was informing the staff and parents about my upcoming surgery. Once again I decided a little bit of humor could help an otherwise dismal piece of news. I sat at my computer to compose the email, starting with the subject line that read, "getting something off of my chest." I proceeded to share the date of the surgery, the dates of recovery, and the date of my return. I thanked them in advance for their understanding, patience, and kindness. Then I pushed the send button before I had time to question and rethink my words.

When the morning of the surgery arrived, my husband and I shuffled the kids off to school before driving to the hospital. The procedure was considered outpatient so I would be released after the surgery and recovery was complete. I filled out all the necessary forms and was in the process of writing a check for the copay portion for the surgery. It was difficult to write such a large check. In order to write this check, I had to dip into my emergency account, which had been created by many years of penny pinching and coupon clipping. As I filled in the blanks on the check, I tried to convince myself that this was the exact situation the emergency fund was created. Even though writing the check was painful, I knew not writing the check would be deadly.

I was quickly prepped and ready, but I had to wait an extremely long time in a holding area. I didn't complain because the nurses there were fabulous. I felt like I was at a five star resort instead of a hospital. They covered me with heated blankets, brought me magazines, and gave me a constant supply of reassurance.

The scheduled time for the surgery came and went, yet no doctor had shown up. By now even the nurses had started to verbalize their concern about the situation. Suddenly the curtain surrounding my hospital bed swooshed open as if it were a stage curtain on the opening night of a Broadway play. There stood the plastic surgeon dressed in his light blue scrubs.

"I am glad to see you. We were beginning to worry," I shared with him.

"Sorry about that. I'm running late today. I do have a little bad news for you. The breast specialist won't be assisting me today," he explained.

That didn't seem like her to back out of the surgery without telling me so I asked why she wouldn't be here.

"I take responsibility for this situation," he admitted. "No one from my office contacted her about your surgery."

"Now what?" I responded in a slightly angry voice.

"I can complete the surgery without her. I've done several of these," he tried to reassure me. "You do have the option of not having the surgery today, and we can reschedule with the specialist for another date. The choice is totally up to you."

"You do have an operating room and an anesthesiologist scheduled, right?" I asked in a sarcastic tone. I was mad at him. He had sabotaged my strategic plan. He was my wild card, the young doctor with the new ideas. The breast specialist was my ace in the hole with her many years of experience and her calm, cool demeanor. My plan was to have the best of both worlds, but now here I was on surgery day hoping I wasn't stuck with the joker.

"Let's go ahead and do it," I said. "I just want to get this over with."

"Great, let's get started. We haven't discussed the final outcome of the surgery. What size breasts do you want? Some women who are large breasted prefer to have no breasts after the surgery," he told me.

I assured him that wasn't the case with me. I still wanted to have nice curves. I still wanted to look like a lady. Once we agreed on a size, he retrieved a black Sharpie marker from his pocket, flipped off the lid, and began sketching on my chest.

That's a permanent marker. Are you kidding me? Little did I know it wasn't going to matter. The marker lines would be removed along with the skin and breast tissue during the surgery.

When I peered down at my chest, I saw several solid and dotted lines, which reminded me of a pirate's treasure map. I searched but unfortunately I never did find the "x" marking the location of the hidden treasure. Perhaps the treasure was the cluster of cancer cells not hidden in an illusive treasure chest, but ironically in my physical chest.

Before the surgery I felt like I was at a five star resort instead of a hospital. The kind and caring nurses had catered to my every need. After the surgery I felt like I had suddenly been transported to an Army boot camp. As soon as I opened my eyes, the nurses began barking orders at me without a please or thank you.

"Sit up! Eat these ice chips! Sip this water!" they commanded. Still groggy from the anesthesia, I complied like a programmed robot. Thank goodness my husband Greg was there to hold my hand and whisper kind words to me.

As the anesthesia began to wear off I became more coherent, and Greg decided it was a good time to explain what had happened during the surgery. He felt the operation had taken an extraordinary long time. He thought since there was only one doctor instead of two performing the procedure, it was taking longer. Periodically a nurse was sent out to inform him about the progress of the surgery. The tissue had been removed, but the doctor was having trouble putting me back together. There were complications with restoring the blood supply to the right side. Some of the tissue had died and needed to be removed.

"As a result, you may be a little lopsided," Greg informed me.

I gazed down at my chest but couldn't tell a difference. I was wrapped in gauze, bandages, and some kind of compression garment. Lopsided. At this point I didn't care. At least this part of the ordeal was over.

The doctor came in to repeat what Greg had just told me. Then he signed my release papers. I was anxious to leave the boot camp and drill sergeants. Soon we were in the car heading home.

"How do you feel?" Greg asked me on the ride home.

"I know this may sound strange, but I feel so light, especially my shoulders. It's like the old saying, 'A weight has been taken off of my shoulders.'" Only in this case it really is true!" I shared.

For the next two days, the prescription pain medications I was taking turned me into a zombie who slept on the couch. Reality was distorted. Objects seemed further away than they actually were. The voices from the TV and radio spoke in slow motion. A coworker stopped by one evening to deliver flowers from the staff. I know I answered the door and spoke with her for a few minutes, but what either one of us said was a total mystery to me.

After two days of zombie living, I ditched the prescription meds for some simple over the counter stuff. It controlled my pain, but allowed me to function as a normal human being. I healed very quickly, and before I knew it, I was ready to return to work.

It was a Monday morning. I arrived early as usual. I read over the notes Joy had left as to what she had accomplished with the kids. Then I anxiously awaited the arrival of the students. I positioned myself in the hall just outside of our classroom ready to give and receive my morning dose of high fives, fist bumps, and hugs. When the first students appeared around the corner, I could tell they were unsure how to greet me. It was as if I was made of glass, and they were afraid they were going to break me.

My solution was to outstretch my arms in a gesture inviting them to give me a hug. I was cushioned with large amounts of gauze and bandages. There was no way they were going to hurt me. Soon a line of students waiting for a hug formed in front of me. In an effort to conserve time, I yelled, "Group hug!" A stampede of students rushed toward me. There were arms and smiles everywhere. Laughter and giggles echoed through the hall as we swayed back and forth in our own little world. It was a moment of happiness I will never forget.

Chapter 4
It's Not About You

Before my surgery, I often interacted with the kids at recess as a supervisor and also as a partial participant in their games. We had several adults out on the playground during recess to help supervise the students, so I felt comfortable periodically joining their activities. I usually did this when there were cases of bickering and arguing about fairness and rules. A refresher on the rules and a little modeling of fair play actually went a long way.

Often I was the permanent pitcher in the kickball game because the kids always argued about who would play that position. I was the line judge at the foursquare courts, and I twirled the rope for the girls who jumped rope. After my surgery, my new body made me feel like a giddy school girl because that was the last time I had been flat chested. Now I wanted to be an active participant in the recess games.

Two weeks after my return to work, I felt physically strong enough to join the kickball game. I walked onto the field but stopped at home plate instead of continuing on to the pitcher's mound.

"Mrs. Pottorff, what are you doing? You're always the pitcher," a kid asked.

"Not today. Find somebody else to pitch. Today I'm kicking and running the bases," I said as I raised my hands up in the air with two peace signs symbolizing my team's anticipated victory.

Of course an argument followed as to who would be the pitcher. I did the old pick a number between one and twenty trick, and soon we had somebody on the mound.

I have always encouraged kids to be strategic thinkers in a variety of activities whether it was academics, social situations, or sports. Today I thought I'd model strategic thinking for them for the millionth time. As a group they were great at catching pop flies, but if you kept your kick on the ground, they could not field the ball if their lives depended on it. Every time I was up, I kicked a ground ball near third base, which gave me plenty of time to run to first base at the opposite side of the diamond. It was freeing to actually run. It hadn't done it in years. Each time I made it to a base I jumped up and down in celebration, yelling at my teammates to "kick me home!" Recess seemed to fly by. There was a lot less arguing and a lot more laughing on the kickball diamond that week.

My escapades on the kickball field increased my confidence and led me to the foursquare courts the following week. Usually I was the line judge, but this time I confidently took a square on the court. This action was met with shocked looks from the kids who considered themselves foursquare professionals.

"When was the last time you played foursquare?" a brave student asked as if he was a detective interrogating a criminal.

"I think I was an elementary school student," I answered nonchalantly.

"That was a looooong time ago. Are you sure you remember how to play?" a girl questioned.

"Thanks for your vote of confidence, but I think once I start playing, it will all come back to me," I reassured the kids.

Obviously, they weren't convinced because the still skeptical students felt the need to review the rules of the game in order to insure some level of success for me.

"We do 'cherry bombs and baby drops.' You know that, right?" a student shared in an effort to intimidate me.

"Come on, guys. You're taking all the fun out of this. Let's just play," I finally said. I may have sounded positive and confident on the outside, but on the inside I really thought they were going to whoop on me. They had quick reflexes, speed, agility, and experience. I had . . . to tell the truth, I didn't know what I had. I guess I had a new body and a newfound desire to play and have fun. Much to my surprise, they didn't crush me after all. It all did come back to me. They could "cherry bomb and baby drop" me all they wanted. It didn't matter because I had a simple strategy. If a player was at the front of his/her square, I hit the ball to the back and vice versa. I wasn't a stellar player, but I held my own. I was proud and happy with my level of play.

After a week of foursquare, I decided to move on to jump rope. I often twirled one end of the rope so more girls could have turns at jumping. On this particular day, instead of grabbing an end of the rope, I positioned myself in the line to jump. Even though none of the girls questioned my intention, I was questioning my action. I was always horrible at jumping rope, even as a kid. What was I thinking? What was I trying to prove? As each girl took her turn, I inched my way closer to the rope and closer to what I was convinced was going to be a "fall flat on your face" failure. By the time it was my turn, I had completely talked myself out of any form of confidence I may have originally had, but I wasn't ready to give up before I even started. I decided to ask the girls for help.

"I don't think I remember how to jump in. Can you girls help me?" I asked. Of course, I could have had the girls stop the rope, then stand beside it, and jump on the first twirl. But that was "baby stuff," and we all knew it. I wanted to jump in while the rope was twirling like everyone else did. I had decided if I was going to fail, I was going fail with style.

"Just twirl the rope, and the rest of you tell me when to jump in," I instructed them.

On the first try I stepped on the rope. The rope whacked me in the head on the next attempt. The third try was magical, and the jump in was successful! The girls began to chant, "Cinderella dressed in yellow. Went upstairs to kiss a fellow. How many kisses did she get?" Each jump I made after that counted as a kiss. I made it to twenty-five kisses before stepping on the rope and ending my turn. *Twenty-five kisses! Not bad for an old broad.*

Not only was I feeling differently physically, but I also felt differently emotionally. I felt grateful the cancer had been detected so early. I knew I would always fear that it would return, but I also knew I had been given a second chance. That second chance gave me a new perspective on life. Somehow the sky seemed bluer. The grass seemed greener. Food tasted better, and my friends were sweeter. Little things that used to annoy me now didn't seem to be worth the worry. Once again, I was looking for the up side of the situation again. I had anticipated my physical recovery would have taken several weeks, yet I was playing kickball, foursquare, and jumping rope. I could have spent my time worrying about a reoccurrence, but instead I was enjoying each day with a new appreciation.

Life was clicking along in a positive manner until my older sister Barb planted an idea in my head that would haunt me until I took some form of action regarding it. Barb had battled melanoma for many years. She was continually having chunks of her flesh removed, but she never complained. In fact, one of the many characteristic traits I admired about her was she didn't grumble about her problems. Instead she searched for solutions. To her, cancer was a problem and the solution was to raise money to find a cure. She became very active in American Cancer Society. She was a true crusader who organized the local Relay for Life, golf tournaments, auctions, and bake sales. She sold everything from t-shirts to daffodils to raise money to find a cure. Through her own experience and her interaction with other cancer survivors, she had gained extensive knowledge about the disease and how it affects the lives of so many people.

Throughout my life, Barb had always been more than just a sister. She was my friend and my mentor. After my diagnosis, her role as a mentor had taken on a whole new meaning. Shortly after my surgery, she began sending me gifts with encouraging notes. First, she sent a cute, pink watch. Then a pink ribbon lapel pin arrived. Next it was a "Fight Like a Girl" t-shirt.

I loved the look of the shirt. It was very sporty and unique with its black background, hot pink boxing gloves, and lettering. What I loved the most about the shirt was the profit from it was being donated to cancer research and to help people who were struggling to pay for cancer treatments like surgery, chemotherapy, radiation, and medications. I knew not everyone had an emergency fund like I had used to pay my copay bills. Many people face financial ruin because they are unable to pay for these life saving treatments.

As much as I liked the shirt and what it stood for, I just couldn't bring myself to wear it. I wasn't ashamed of having cancer, but I didn't want to advertise that fact. To me this was a personal journey not a public one. In my fantasy world I would have preferred to have the surgery, take a few days off, and return to work without anyone knowing about my diagnosis. But I worked with a group of sharp kids and adults. I knew when I returned from surgery somebody was going to notice I was missing a couple of body parts, so I had to share my story not only with the staff and students but the entire community. That situation was hard enough, and now my sister expected me to wear a shirt, which told the world I had breast cancer. I didn't think I was up to the challenge.

When Barb called that week to check in with me, she asked if I liked the shirt. Of course, I thanked her for her kind and thoughtful gift stating how much I loved the design and the cause it represented.

"I just don't think I can wear it," I explained. " I'm not one to draw attention to myself. It's like a billboard asking for people to feel sorry for me because I have breast cancer. I don't want to wear pink for the rest of my life or to have a breast cancer survivor license plate on my car. I just want to be normal. I just want things to go back to the way they were."

"Listen to me," she countered. "Hasn't your life changed since your diagnosis?"

"Yes," I told her. Then I explained how I had been physically feeling better, and on the emotional level I felt so grateful for the simple things in life.

"Those are common responses," she shared with me. "You do realize your life is never going to be the same, right?"

Silence. I had to think about what she was saying for a minute.

"Yes, I understand that," I admitted.

"If you understand that then you are ready for the next step," she said.

"What's that?" I asked.

"It's a realization that this situation really isn't about you. You are a cancer survivor for a reason. It's to help other people with their journeys," she clarified.

Again, silence. I knew she was right. She was always right. That's why she was the big sister, and I was the little sister. She was the mentor, and I was the mentee. She was the veteran cancer survivor, and I was the rookie. I thanked her again for the shirt and words of wisdom then hung up the phone.

I knew I needed time to "chew" on the idea Barb had presented to me. I knew I needed to be strategic regarding my mental outlook on this situation as well as my actions regarding it. While allowing myself time to think, I hung the shirt in my closet knowing I would eventually wear it in public when the time was right.

Two weeks later the planets must have aligned because I felt like it was time to wear the shirt. It was a Saturday morning. I was headed to Wal-Mart to shop for groceries and a few other items. I slipped on the "Fight Like a Girl" t-shirt, black yoga pants, and a pair of sporty black and pink sneakers.

"I can do this," I told myself as I grabbed my purse, car keys, and headed out the door.

As I was getting out of my car at the Wal-Mart parking lot, a lady was getting into her car in the space next to mine.

"Nice shirt," she said to me before shutting her car door and driving away. That wasn't so bad. I truly thought that was going to be my one and only encounter regarding the shirt for the day. Wow, was I naïve.

I was in the housewares department when a young man in his early thirties pulled his shopping cart next to mine.

"I couldn't help but notice your cool shirt," he began. "Are you a cancer survivor?"

"Yes, I am."

"My sister has been recently diagnosed with breast cancer. In fact, it was just last week. She is pretty scared. Our entire family is scared."

I shared with him that being scared and frightened is a natural response for everyone involved because the diagnosis is so shocking. Then I explained a little bit about my journey.

"Can I ask you where you got that shirt?" he continued. "I think I would like to get one for my sister. I like the message it sends. It might be just what she needs to change her attitude from fear to fight."

I told him my sister, who was also a cancer survivor, had sent it to me. I explained he could order one online by looking up Fight Like a Girl.

"Thanks," he replied. " Thanks for taking the time to talk to me." Then we wished each other well and went our separate ways. I could tell by the change in his demeanor during our short conversation, that I had helped him somehow. I also knew in my heart that he had helped me as well. He helped me to realize wearing the shirt wasn't a way to draw attention to myself, or a way to gain pity from people. It had a whole different purpose. It was an icebreaker, a conversation starter. It told people I had something in common with them . . .cancer, and I wasn't afraid to talk about it. No one would have known that about me if I hadn't worn the shirt.

I was coming to grips with this concept in the parking lot. I had loaded my car and was returning my shopping cart to the cart coral when an older woman stopped me. Three of her family members quickly joined her.

"I love your shirt. I am a breast cancer survivor, too. I have been for over fifteen years," she proudly explained. "How long has it been for you?"

"I was diagnosed just a few months ago," I told her.

"You're going to be fine. Just like me," she assured me. "Here's one thing I want you to know. We must never give up trying to find the cure for cancer. Remember that."

"I agree."

Her family members then joined the conversation explaining her battle with cancer in more detail. She had been through surgery, chemotherapy, radiation, and medications. She had been a tireless advocate for other people who had cancer, and she was on a mission to raise money in order to find the cure. They ended the conversation by sharing how proud they were of her. I was so moved by her story that in that impromptu moment, I asked the lady if I could give her a hug. After we embraced she said to me, "Don't give up the fight," as she pointed to my shirt.

"I won't," I assured her.

When I returned home I called Barb to tell her about my Wal-Mart experiences and the magic of the t-shirt.

"You were right," I told her. "I'm just beginning to realize this situation reaches beyond me. There is more to this fight than just my personal battle against cancer. There is a fight going on that is much bigger than me, much bigger than even my realm of thinking. I just need to figure out how I fit into the big picture. How do I fit into the battle plan?"

After my conversation with Barb ended, I replayed my experiences at Wal-Mart in my mind. It isn't unusual for complete strangers to talk to me. It happens to me quite often. In fact, my husband refers to me as "the goof magnet." People most often speak to me while we are waiting in check out lines. After I have finished a conversation with someone, my husband often asks, "Do you know that person?"

"No, but I do now," is my usual response.

Talking to complete strangers is a common occurrence for me. What was unusual on this particular day was the number of these interactions. One interaction about my shirt would have been normal, but three? It seemed like God was sending me a message. Little did I know it at the time, but this was just a foreshadowing of God speaking to me in numerous ways; through situations, through other people, through visions, through words which whispered in my imagination, through an aching feeling in my gut and in my heart. At times I fought His will because I was afraid. I was afraid to take a chance. I was afraid I didn't have the strength, intelligence, character, or charisma to succeed. Basically, I was afraid of failing, but once I gave in to God's will, to God's plan for me, I felt at peace.

I think we all have experienced times in our lives when we have felt the need to reinvent ourselves. Sometimes it is by choice, and at other times we are forced to change because of circumstances we have no control over. My body had definitely been changed by the surgery. My spirit had been changed in that I felt healthier, energized, and grateful for each day I had been given. Slowly my soul was transforming through the realization that cancer was changing my life, and I, in turn, was using those changes to benefit others. So often in life when I felt the need to reinvent myself, I felt as if my life was a puzzle, and I meticulously took it apart piece by piece. But I didn't put it back together in the same way. What would be the point? Not only did I reassemble the puzzle in a new and different way, I also completed the task with God's help. It has always been God's grace and guiding hand that has made my life's puzzle richer, deeper, more meaningful, interesting, intriguing, and beautiful beyond my imagination. This situation was no different. I knew in my heart God had a plan for me, which would be revealed throughout my cancer journey. I just needed to trust Him, and to commit my entire being, body and soul, to do His will.

Chapter 5
Yahoo! I Have A Tattoo!

My transformation of body and soul continued over the next few months. Physically my body continued to heal. Soon I no longer needed the gauze, which covered my incisions. The next step was to have the stitches removed. Then I no longer needed the wrap around bandage. I was down to just wearing my compression garment.

I had met with my assigned oncologist at the Rocky Mountain Cancer Center in Colorado Springs. He informed me that since the cancer was at the earliest stage I would not need chemotherapy, but he recommended radiation treatments. He gave me a prescription for tamoxifen, which at the time was a drug breast cancer patients took to ward off a reoccurrence. I would be taking the drug daily for the next five years.

I was now the proud owner of three tattoos, which sounded much more "buff" than what it really was. The tattoos were three small dots about the size of a period at the end of a sentence. These dots would be used to line up the radiation machine on my body. I had one dot on each side of my rib cage and one in the middle of my chest. I was simply waiting to get the okay from the plastic surgeon that my incisions had healed enough so I could begin the radiation treatments.

Finally, the day of my last appointment with the plastic surgeon arrived. I waited patiently in the exam room. He knocked on the door then quickly entered. I was surprised to see he had a cell phone tucked between his right shoulder and ear. Unfortunately, the sound must have been set at the maximum volume because I could hear every word the person on the other end was saying. It was another doctor, and they were discussing a patient they shared. The plastic surgeon continued the phone conversation throughout my entire exam, which I felt was very hurtful and extremely unprofessional. It made me feel like a body and not a person. I simply wanted the examination to be over so I put up with the doctor's rude behavior. In a matter of minutes he gave me two thumbs up then he exited the room still talking on the phone about a recent golf game the two doctors had shared.

"I guess two thumbs up means I can start my radiation treatments?" I asked the nurse when she entered the room a few minutes later.

"That's what it says here," she informed me as she glanced through a stack of papers on the clipboard in her hand.

I signed several forms on the clipboard she handed me. Then I dressed, left the exam room, the office, and vowed to never return there again.

By now it was late November. Thanksgiving had come and gone, but to tell the truth, every day seemed like Thanksgiving to me. I was so grateful to be healthy. My next step was to schedule an appointment with the radiologist who would manage the treatment stage of my recovery.

On the day of the appointment with the radiologist, I checked in at the desk, then found a comfortable spot on a couch to wait with a good book I had stuffed in my purse. The buzz of so many people speaking in the waiting area made me realize the number of people who have cancer must be staggering. Some people I could surmise, by their physical appearance, had the dreaded disease. Their pale complexions, thin bodies, and hairless heads were clues. Then there were people like me who had no outward signs of the disease. One thing I realized during my people watching was cancer doesn't discriminate. It doesn't matter about age, race, sex, or your income bracket. Cancer can attack anyone.

Suddenly, there was a flurry of activity in the north corner of the waiting room. I looked up from my book to see a staff member open the door to what I assumed was a storage closet. A bald cancer patient was standing next to her. They both stepped inside the room leaving the door open. I was right. It was a storage closet, but not an ordinary storage closet. It was filled with wigs. There were wigs attached to foam heads sitting on shelves, which reached from the floor to the ceiling. There had to be hundreds of wigs of every hair color and style imaginable. The hairless woman took a seat in a black, leather chair, which you would normally see in a beauty parlor. The floor to ceiling mirror across from the chair completed the salon look. The staff member began selecting wigs from the shelves and placing them in front of the patient.

"It's very impressive, isn't it?" a beautiful, dark haired woman asked as she sat down next to me.

"Yes. It's amazing. My mom used to help people acquire wigs when they were going through chemotherapy treatments, but she never had a very large selection," I responded.

"I am the Nurse Navigator for your case," she said. Then she introduced herself and explained what was going to happen during my appointment. "Follow me and let's get started."

Soon I was in an exam room where I met the radiologist who would be in charge of my case. I immediately felt comfortable with him. He was a tall, thin man who, even though he had white hair, had a very young face. What an interesting dichotomy I thought. He was very thorough about explaining how the radiation would kill any stray cancer cells left from the surgery. Considering how much tissue had been removed during my surgery, I doubted there were any "stray" cancer cells. In my book, the radiation was a precautionary measure. It was what I refer to as CYB or "cover your behind." This way my doctors could say they had done everything to prevent the cancer from recurring. That was okay with me. CYB is actually a good plan, especially in this circumstance.

After a quick exam, the radiologist asked me if I had any questions. Just to continue to focus on the positive, I asked him how the early detection of my cancer would affect my treatment and recovery. I think I already knew the answer, but I wanted to hear it from him. He explained early detection was the reason I was doing just radiation and not chemotherapy.

The nurse navigator seemed to assume my positive attitude meant I wasn't taking the situation seriously, so she chimed in, "But let's get this straight. Even though your cancer is at the earliest stage, you do have cancer, and you need to act like you have cancer."

What in the world did that mean? I had watched my father, brother, sister, and countless friends and relatives deal with cancer. My conclusion, after watching them travel this journey, was that each person deals with cancer in his or her own individual way. Gilda Radner once said, "Cancer is probably the most unfunny thing in the world, but I'm a comedian, and cancer couldn't stop me from seeing humor in what I was going through." If Gilda Radner could find humor in a disease that eventually took her life, certainly I could focus on the positive outcomes of having cancer. If that was what it was going to take for me to travel this journey, then so be it. There is no right or wrong way to be a cancer patient. There is only YOUR way. It is as individual as each person on the planet. So I decided to ignore the nurse navigator's comment. She could navigate someone else's cancer journey. I would navigate my own.

I left the exam room and headed to the scheduling department. Once again I was surprised by the lack of urgency in my treatment. It would be a week before they could fit me into the schedule. It was then I realized there must be so many people who needed to be treated for cancer. I would have to wait until someone finished his or her radiation treatments before I could begin mine. I tried to look for the positive . . . the up side of the situation. At least I would have more time to heal. I was able to take a time slot later in the day at three. This meant

I wouldn't have to leave school until two, which I thought was also a positive.

I had one more stop before leaving the hospital that day. The radiologist had told me I would need to obtain two items before beginning my radiation treatments, deodorant without aluminum, which could be purchased at a grocery store, and a special lotion, which would prevent my skin from drying out. The lotion could only be purchased at the hospital's gift shop/pharmacy so that's where I headed. When I couldn't find the lotion on the shelves, I asked the pharmacist for help. He quickly informed me the lotion was out of stock. In fact, it was in such demand that it was always out of stock, but he would gladly put my name on a waiting list and would call me when the next shipment arrived. He handed me a clipboard with a huge list of names and phone numbers. I added my information. As I handed the clipboard back to him, I asked about the price of the lotion. His response made my jaw drop. It was extremely expensive. *The stuff must be imported from another universe.* I thought to myself as I exited the shop and headed toward the parking garage.

Time flew by quickly, and soon my first radiation treatment was only days away. By now it was early December. My first appointment was actually a practice session used to line up my tattoos with the machine and make necessary adjustments. Because this was more time consuming than a regular radiation treatment, it was scheduled after the last appointment of the day on a Friday. I arrived to an empty waiting room, took a seat, and nervously thumbed through several magazines. Suddenly a technician appeared before me holding a clipboard.

"Are you someone's driver?" she asked.

I looked up from the magazine I was holding with a startled look on my face. "No, I'm a patient," I answered.

"Oh, I am sorry," she said. "You must be Pam."

"Yes, that's me," I explained.

"Follow me," she instructed. She led me to a dimly lit treatment room where I met the team of technicians who would be in charge of my radiation treatments. Soon I was on the treatment table with the large machinery looming around me. The technicians were lining up my tattoos with the machine when I was hit with a sudden panic attack. My chest tightened, constricting my breath. I closed my eyes in an effort to regain my composure, but all I could see was my body lying on the treatment table. My outstretched arms reminded me of Jesus on the cross. Suddenly, I was frightened. My heart was throbbing quickly and pounding against my chest. My eyes flickered open.

"I need to sit up for a minute," I told the technician.

"No, problem," she assured me. "Take your time. You're our last patient today so take as long as you need."

Maybe I had been physically "held together" with stitches, gauze, and bandages. Maybe I had been emotionally held together with my faith and never-ending quest to find the positive in each step of this journey. For some reason, at this moment in

61

time, I could no longer hold it together. I was falling apart. I could feel all my worry, concern, and fears welling up inside me on the verge of spilling out, but I refused to let that happen. I decided to refocus my energy by singing one of my favorite hymns in my head.

"Be not afraid. I go before you always. Come follow me, and I will give you rest." As these words echoed and repeated in my mind, my breathing returned to normal, and I felt a sense of peace wash over my body. The words helped me remember no matter what I faced in life; Christ had gone before me, leading the way, making a path for me to follow, if only I would trust Him. Maybe that was why I had the vision of Christ on the cross. He had gone before me, so that I would have nothing to fear. Christ's death on the cross was a sacrifice made for others. Maybe my sister Barb was right. This journey wasn't about me. It was about helping others. I needed to let go of my selfish ways before I could continue on this journey

"I trust you, Lord," my voice whispered over and over in my head. I took in a deep breath. Then I let go. I let go of all of my fears. I let go of thinking only about me. I let go of all of the air in my lungs, and I felt at peace. I laid back down on the table. "Okay, I'm ready," I told the technicians.

When I arrived home that afternoon, I decided I needed something to occupy my mind during each of my radiation treatments. I thought I could sing a favorite song in my head like I had done today during my anxiety attack, but somehow that didn't seem right. It would be only a matter of minutes when the radiation would be zapped into my body, which wouldn't be enough time to complete a song. I needed something short, simple, to the point, yet purposeful and beautiful. I needed a prayer, but not just any ordinary prayer. I needed a prayer specifically for this situation. Not a prayer about me, or my needs, but a prayer for other people with cancer. I didn't think such a prayer already existed so I decided to create this prayer myself. Suddenly, a little self-doubt began to creep into my thoughts. *Am I even capable of writing a prayer? Of course I am! Praying is just talking to God, and writing is just talking on paper. I can do this!* I went to the bedroom and rummaged through the nightstand until I found my journal. I opened the pages. I opened my heart to God, and the words began to flow out onto the page.

Dear God, Please help all the people in the world who suffer from cancer. Please help them physically and emotionally. Please help the patients and their families deal with this dreaded disease. Please help the doctors and researchers find the cause and the cure for cancer and wipe it off the face of the Earth. Please end the suffering caused by cancer and help people regain their health so that they may continue to do Your will. Amen.

I read over my prayer several times, and decided I liked it. As I stared at the words on the page, I decided today was an important day. God was speaking to me, loud and clear. He spoke to me with the vision I experienced when I was on the treatment table. He spoke to me with the gift of words, which became my original prayer. All I had to do was to be open to His messages. I needed to open my heart, open my mind, be at peace, and be receptive. It seemed simple, yet it seemed complicated at the same time. What if people found out I was receiving messages from God? Would they think I was crazy? Who cares! If God was communicating with me, that was a gift! I decided I should be grateful not doubtful. Besides, why should I care about what other people thought? I cared more about what God thought and about what I felt. *Let go. Let go. Let go.* I told myself. *Let go and trust in God.*

I mixed up a batch of chocolate chip cookie dough. Miraculous as it may sound, I barely ate any of it. (Okay, maybe a couple of tablespoons.) I didn't eat it because I didn't make it for stress relief. I had another purpose for it in mind. On the drive home, I realized I had been doing a good job of seeing the positive side of each challenge my cancer journey had presented, but I began to wonder if I could actually create positive situations rather than just waiting for them to happen. I decided to start with the radiation technicians. Certainly, they had thankless jobs. They worked long hours, yet they were gentle, patient, and thoughtful. I had found over the years that simple gestures like a few kind words, a handwritten note, or a homemade gift are often the most appreciated forms of gratitude because they come from your heart. I had decided to bring this group of wonderful ladies sweet treats each day I had a treatment. The cookies were my first installment of my plan. I couldn't help smiling as I carefully placed a dozen cookies in a festive

Christmas cellophane gift bag, tying a red ribbon to secure the top. I placed the bag of delicious treats in the freezer until I could retrieve it on Monday morning. The good news was I still had a dozen cookies left to serve as dessert after our evening meal.

"Are these all the cookies we have?" my daughter questioned as I sat the plate of chocolate chip delicacies in the center of the table after dinner. "Did you eat the dough again?"

"No, I did not. At least not very much of it," I admitted. "I'm taking a dozen cookies to the radiation technicians on Monday, but there's still plenty for us to enjoy."

"Why are you taking them cookies? You don't even know them," she queried.

"Hmmmmm. Let me think about that for a minute. Could it be that they are possibly saving my life?" I answered.

"Mom, you are so dramatic," she replied as she grabbed several cookies, rolled her eyes then headed to her room.

I am the one who is dramatic? You have got to be kidding.

Early Saturday morning, my phone rang. It was my sister Barb calling to check on me. I was thankful the call gave me a much-needed break from my Saturday housekeeping chores. Our conversation began as usual with Barb updating me on all the news from our hometown, but inevitably it led to the "cancer conversation."

"When do you start your radiation treatments?" Barb inquired even though she already knew the answer to her question.

"Monday."

"Do you feel like you are ready?"

"Well, my doctors say I'm healed. I've got my tattoos, and I went through a trial run yesterday so yes. I think I am ready."

"You don't sound ready. Here's something I want you to do. Did you receive a list of dates for your radiation treatments?"

"Yes, on sheets that look like calendar pages. They were in a folder of information the radiation technicians gave me yesterday," I replied as if remembering out loud.

"Perfect. I want you to put those calendar pages on your refrigerator so you can see them every day. When you complete a treatment, come home and mark that day off the calendar pages on your refrigerator door. It is going to give you a sense of accomplishment. You'll be able to see how many treatments you've completed and how many you have left. Can you do that for me? Can you put the calendar pages up?"

"Yes, I can do that. In fact, that is a great idea."

"This ain't my first time around the block, you know. Hey Sis, you've got this! I don't mean the calendar thing. I mean the whole cancer thing. You've got this. You can do this!"

I swallowed a lump in my throat before I responded. "Thanks, Barb. I needed that. I especially needed to hear it from you. I love you."

"I love you, too," she responded before we both ended the call.

I immediately went into the master bedroom and scrounged around the drawer of my nightstand until I found the gray pocket folder one of the radiation technicians had given me the day before. I ruffled through the sheets of paper in the pockets until I found the calendar pages listing all of my radiation treatments. I transported the calendar pages to the kitchen where I hung them in a predominate place on the refrigerator with the largest magnets I could find. Now I was ready. Let the radiation begin.

DECEMBER 2011

SUN	MON	TUES	WED	THURS	FRI	SAT
				1	2	3
4	5	6	7	8	9	10
11	12	13	14	15	16	17
18	19	20	21	22	23	24
25	26	27	28	29	30	31

Chapter 6
The Power of
Positive Thinking

Not only had I decided to set up a positive
situation for the radiation technicians by bringing
them treats each day, but I was also developing a
way to set up a positive situation for my students as
well. A half-day substitute teacher always comes
in at noon, but I didn't need to leave school for my
radiation treatments until two o'clock. At first I
was unsure what to do with the time between Joy's
arrival and my departure. Once I had decided to
create positive situations, the solution seemed so
logical and simple.

Unfortunately in the United States of America,
one of the greatest nations on the planet, teachers
aren't given the resources they need to educate their
students. The resource I most desperately lacked
was time. A perfect example of this was at the end
of every school year in the district in which I
worked, every elementary school teacher was
required to give each student a one-on-one reading
test. The students needed to read the passages on
the test out loud so I could record their errors.
Portions of the questions, as well as the answers,
were completed orally. My dilemma was if I tested
students in the classroom, everyone would hear the
passages, the questions, and the answers. If I took
students out in the hall to administer the tests, the
rest of the class would be unsupervised. Each
spring, the school district would pay for a substitute
teacher to be in my room for two days so I could

administer the tests out of the classroom, but that was never nearly enough time. Each year I would call in sick for a couple of days, but still show up for work. There would be a substitute teacher in my classroom while I gave the tests in the hall. My husband would often chastise me for giving up my precious sick days, but I couldn't think of any other options.

"Besides," I told my husband. "You have to do the right thing when it comes to kids." He couldn't argue with that.

Since it was only December, not all the kids were ready to take the end of the year reading test, but the kids in my top two reading groups were very capable of completing it. They were reading above and beyond the third grade level. So I decided to eat lunch and plan with Joy from noon until when the students came in from recess at 12:30 then I would take kids out to the hall to administer the reading tests until my departure time. These were the advanced students so I knew I could pull them out of class for a few minutes, and they could assimilate back into the classroom with no problems. This use of the time seemed like a stroke of genius to me so I implemented it as soon as my radiation treatments began.

Monday rolled around. The first day of radiation treatments had arrived, and I was prepared. I had my buff tattoos to line up the radiation equipment. I had completed a trial run treatment. Joy was ready and willing to sub for me every afternoon. I had talked to the bus driver who would drop Landon off at the designated bus stop so I could pick him up after my treatments. But was I ready emotionally? That was the looming question. There was only one way to find out . . . just do it. Just go through a treatment.

The morning seemed like any other Monday morning with the exception that the students were very quiet, which was uncharacteristic for them as a group. Joy arrived at noon. Joy and I ate lunch together and discussed the plans for the afternoon. She taught, and I tested students in the hall until 2 p.m., the bewitching hour. My heart was racing as I put away the testing materials and packed my canvas backpack with papers to grade. It was then that I realized I had left my grade book in the classroom. This new development quickly sabotaged my plan of sneaking out through the door in the front lobby.

I peaked my head in the classroom doorway. Joy was at the front of the room teaching a math lesson. She shot me a reassuring glance and said, "Oh, we thought you were gone."

"I forgot my grade book," I announced as I tiptoed across the classroom as if I were a devious cat burglar. I grabbed the grade book from my desk, stuffed it into my backpack, and quickly zipped the backpack shut. The room was totally silent, which made the sound of the backpack zipper echo off the walls at an exaggerated volume.

Finally, the silence was broken by an unexpected source. The most mischievous boy in the class popped out of his seat. Walking towards me he exclaimed, "Let me carry your backpack to your car for you, Mrs. Pottorff."

"Thank you," I responded in a shocked tone as I slid the strap of my backpack off my shoulder and handed it to him. His bold, kind comment and gesture had shattered the uncomfortable silence. There were many days when his behavior had tested my patience and drained my energy, but today I was glad he was standing before me. Today he was a true blessing in my life.

As he and I walked to the outside classroom door, other students followed his example with various forms of good-bye and well wishes.

"Good-bye, Mrs. Pottorff."

"We will see you tomorrow."

"We will work hard when you are gone."

"We'll take care of Mrs. Wagner."

Everyone chuckled. We all knew who was taking care of whom. I shot a glance at Joy, and we exchanged smiles. True teachers know the beauty and magic of children. Children wear their hearts on their sleeves. They say whatever pops into their heads without any filters. Kids are honest, simple, and pure. Their concern and sincerity was magical. It transformed me from a frightened, insecure woman who had slithered into her own classroom to retrieve a grade book to a confident, brave lady who was loved and supported by this group of caring kids. Joy knew what I was feeling. Her smile said it all.

I stopped at the outside classroom door, turned, and waved good-bye.

"I'll see you all tomorrow."

I opened the door. The sunlight burst into the room and lit the splendid situation. The backpack-laden student and I stepped onto the sidewalk, and the door clicked shut behind us. There was no going back now.

Soon we were standing at the back of my car. I pushed my key fob to unlock the doors. I opened the back hatch of my small SUV, and my young helper deposited the bulky backpack in the cargo area.

"I want to give you something for helping me today," I said to the boy. I reached inside the plastic container, which was the emergency kit my husband had created for me and grabbed a grape Jolly Rancher candy.

As I handed the piece of candy to the young man, he startled me by reaching out to give me a sincere but clumsy hug. As he patted my back, he mumbled, "You're going to be okay, Mrs. Pottorff." Then he turned, ran across the parking lot without looking for cars, and threw his candy wrapper on the grass outside of our classroom. He knocked on the classroom door until someone let him in then mysteriously disappeared inside.

I stood in disbelief behind my car with the hatch door still open. This was a boy who never hugged anyone. When I greeted the students at the door each morning, he was content with a simple fist bump. He was constantly in trouble for testing the rules and stretching the boundaries. As I stood on the asphalt of the school parking lot, I realized miracles do happen because I had just witnessed one. Cancer was changing my life, but it was at that moment in time that I realized cancer was changing the lives of the people around me.

When I reached the hospital I couldn't find a parking spot. *Great*, I thought to myself. I don't want to be late for my first treatment. I quickly realized it was just my nerves flaring up again. Just breathe. I told myself.

Eventually, I found a parking place and signed in at the desk with plenty of time to spare. As I sauntered to the waiting area, I surveyed the room with an inquisitive eye. Sometimes when I am anxious or afraid I draw into myself and at other times I want to talk. Today I was in the talking mood. The question was who would be willing to talk to me? After surveying the room, I realized this was a multiple-choice question.

Choice A was an elderly gentleman who was slumped over in his wheelchair. A closer glance revealed several tubes connecting to an oxygen tank and an intravenous bag hanging on a hook on the side of his wheelchair. He didn't seem to be a viable choice. For one thing, he was sound asleep.

Choice B was a bald, bird-like young lady sitting at the back of the room with her head buried in a magazine. Clearly, the choice of where she was sitting, how she was hiding her face in the magazine were signs that stated, "Leave me alone!" So I did.

Choice C seemed to be a good option. She was a woman about my age with a beautiful, yellow, silk scarf wrapped around her head. The speed at which she was thumbing through the pages of the magazine she held firmly in her hands, told me she was just looking at the photos and not reading the text. This was something I often did when I was nervous.

"Hi, I'm Pam," I introduced myself as I plopped down in the chair beside her.

"I'm Rosanna," she replied as she looked up from the magazine and smiled.

I took the smile as a good sign so I tried to continue the conversation.

"I love your scarf. It's so classy," I said.

"I have lots of them," she responded. "That's what you do when you don't have any hair."

"Well, whatever the reason, it looks great on you. What are you in for?" I asked with an inquisitive smile.

"Breast cancer, stage three," she answered. "How about you?"

"Breast cancer," I replied without stating the stage because mine was at the beginning stage, and I didn't want to imply that my situation was better than hers.

"Yours must be at the beginning stage judging by your thick head of hair," She responded. She was no dummy. "I assume you didn't have to take any chemo treatments?"

"No, no chemo. Just surgery and radiation," I answered. *JUST surgery and radiation. What was I saying? Good heavens, wasn't that enough? In fact today was JUST my first radiation treatment, and I was JUST a little nervous!*

"I've had radiation treatments for a week, and it hasn't been as bad as I thought it would be," Rosanna volunteered. Perhaps she sensed my nervousness. "I did a round of chemotherapy before this, and that was a different story," she

74

continued. "All I have to say is I will be glad when all of this is over."

We chatted for a few more minutes until a radiation technician came to the waiting area and called Rosanna's name. As she headed back to the treatment area, I said, "I'll see you tomorrow." Little did I know at the time that I would be saying that phrase to her every day for the next several weeks.

"Yeah, I'll see you tomorrow," she called back over her shoulder.

Rosanna. Rosanna. I said her name over and over in my mind so I would remember it. I think I've made a new friend I told myself.

I had barely thumbed through two or three pages of the magazine Rosanna had left with me, when the technician entered the waiting area and called my name. I dropped the magazine on a nearby table and sauntered down the hall to the treatment room. Due to the dose of self-confidence the students had given me, and the soothing conversation Rosanna had offered, my fear had totally dissipated. Ironically, it had taken an hour to drive from work to the hospital, but the treatment itself took approximately five to ten minutes.

There was a card from Barb in the mail when I arrived home. As soon as I deposited my backpack in the living room, I settled myself at the kitchen bar to read the card. It was actually a poem written by Emily Matthews titled Life's Pathways. The beautiful words of the poem traveled like an arrow straight to my heart. It explained how we all travel down the path of life. At times the road is rough,

and we wish it was smoother, but we must always
remember that God is with us every step of the way.
Once we've made it through those rocky patches,
we realize those were the places in the road where
we actually grew and became a better person.

In her beautiful, distinctive handwriting Barb added
this note:

I wiped the salty tears from my cheeks then
dialed Barb's number. I thanked her for the card,
which arrived at the perfect time with the perfect
words of encouragement. I knew I was blessed to
have someone like Barb in my corner, and even
more blessed to have her as my mentor, friend, and
sister. The phone conversation ended with each of
us professing our love for each other then Barb's
final words were, "You can do this!" I hung up the
phone, walked to the refrigerator, and proudly
marked a bright, red X through the day's date on the
December calendar.

"I can do this," I said out loud as a confident
smile spread across my face.

Chapter 7
The Zen of Routine

My life had found a familiar rhythm. I must say there is a certain zen about being in a routine. Having a routine can be structured, calming, and comfortable. I woke each day at 5:30. I taught until noon, tested students until 2 p.m., had my radiation treatment at 3 p.m., picked Landon up at the bus stop, cooked dinner, ate, cleaned up, graded papers until 10 p.m., then went to bed. Repeat every weekday. On Saturdays I talked on the phone with Barb then did laundry and housework. Sundays consisted of church, grocery shopping, writing lesson plans and the class newsletter, grading papers, and off to bed once again.

Within this realm of routine, I was still learning. I was learning about myself, learning about others, learning about my relationship with God, and the relationships with people in my life. Even though I enjoyed the comfort of my routine, there was never a dull moment.

After my encounter with the young man who carried my backpack to my car, I realized how much the students in my class wanted to help me and to be part of my journey. So the kids and I developed a rotation, which allowed a different student each day to carry my backpack to my vehicle. Walking from the school to my car offered excellent one on one time to bond with each child. I let the kids pick the topics of conversation, which ranged from friend problems, to annoying siblings, to after school activities . . . the regular kid stuff.

After my backpack was safely deposited in the back of my SUV, I would reward the student with a Jolly Rancher from my emergency kit then each student would send me off with a friendly, "See you tomorrow, Mrs. Pottorff," accompanied by a hug, high five, or fist bump. With a Jolly Rancher bulging from his or her cheek, the student would run or skip across the parking lot and disappear through the outside door of our classroom. I must admit it was a cheerful, daily send off. I was proud of the kids for adapting to the situation, and for learning to become more independent.

I'd arrive at the cancer center, check in, then spend a few minutes chatting with my new friend, Rosanna, before her radiation treatment. Each day Rosanna wore a different, exotic silk scarf wrapped like a turban around her bald head. She truly looked like a beautiful queen.

"We make quite the pair," I shared with her one day.

"Why is that?" she questioned.

" We have a lot in common," I explained. " First of all, we are both breast cancer survivors. Second, we are both royalty. You look like a queen adorned with your fancy scarves, and I am The Supreme Empress. Well, at least that's what I make the students at school call me."

"You are kidding me, right?" Rosanna laughed. "Do you really make them call you that?"

"I almost hate to admit it, but yes I do. Let me explain. They all have nicknames I've given them. My self-imposed nickname just happens to be The Supreme Empress. I think it demands a certain level of respect. Don't you?" I shared as I held out one of my hands with the pinkie finger extended in a royal gesture.

"What are you The Supreme Empress of, exactly? Your classroom or the entire universe?" Rosanna inquired between fits of giggling.

"The entire universe, of course, darling," I replied as I did what is commonly known as "the beauty queen wave" to the masses of imaginary royal subjects in the room. Trust me, it's not every day that a radiation treatment waiting room is filled with laughter, although maybe it should be.

Through our daily encounters, I found out Rosanna had adult children, but she never mentioned a spouse so I didn't ask. She loved her job and enjoyed her coworkers. Basically, she lived alone, and she was facing her cancer journey alone. I found this amazing because my experience was the total opposite. So many people were on this journey with me . . . my students, their families, staff members, my sister Barb, my family, and friends. I admired Rosanna's strength and courage to travel down this frightening path alone. I was reminded once again that there is no right or wrong way to be a cancer patient. There is only your way! How people move through the cancer process is as unique as each individual. It depends on each person's circumstances, personality, friends, family members, and relationships. When you stop to think about it, there are a multitude of factors to consider. With all that in mind, how could everyone's cancer journey be the same? Impossible.

Each day, my admiration for Rosanna grew. Every day she would stroll dignified and nonchalantly down the hall to her treatment. I would follow a few minutes later, but there was nothing dignified or nonchalant about my trip down the hall. I was just a little, old, schoolmarm dragging a purse stuffed with sweet treats for the radiation techs.

The radiation technicians, all of whom were women, had an interesting schedule. They usually worked in teams of three. There were two treatment rooms with a team assigned to each room. The teams rarely consisted of the same people. Here's why. Approximately every third day, a team member was rotating out to enjoy several days in a row off, while a new person was rotating into the team. After a few days I realized my team of radiation technicians consisted of Rose, Dana, Jennifer, and Rebecca, and I started referring to them as "my peeps."

While the makeup of my radiation treatment team was different, my daily routine was the same. I would arrive in the treatment room and set individually wrapped treats for each technician on the table, which was adjacent to the dressing screen I disrobed behind. The technicians would line up my tattoos with the equipment as I lay on the treatment table. Once that was accomplished I would remain on the table while the techs scurried off with their sweet treats to a nearby lead encased room to control the radiation treatment while enjoying their delicious snacks.

The treatment took only a matter of minutes. I barely had time to recite my daily prayer I had written to calm my nerves. As unusual as it may sound, I became accustomed to the hum of the machine as it placed radiation into my body as well as the snap and click the machine made when it turned on and off. Before I knew it, the technicians arrived back from their lead enclosed hide-a-way laughing and giggling while wiping the sweet treat residue (usually chocolate) from their hands and faces with cheap paper napkins.

As any elementary school teacher in America can testify, the closer it gets to Christmas, the more holiday goodies the students give you. It was now the second week of December, so I already had secured a rather large collection of sweet treats, which included sugar cookies, homemade fudge, loaves of banana bread, Hershey kisses, M & Ms (plain and peanut), Andes mints, Werther's butterscotch candies, boxes of assorted chocolates, and the coveted Rice Krispie treats. I had frozen some of the homemade items to prevent them from becoming stale. Stale holiday goodies, what a waste that would be!

By doing some research, I had found cancer cells, like many of us, love sugar. With that in mind, I decided to cut back on my sugar intake, which left me with the problem of what to do with the incoming holiday goodies from my students. I had decided to take treats to the radiation technicians each day as a way to thank them, so sharing my goodies with the technicians seemed to be the perfect solution.

Every evening after dinner, I would gaze in wonder upon my "sugar stash," then select delightful morsels for each member on my radiation team. I would wrap the delicacies in plastic wrap tied with colorful, holiday curling ribbon so that each team member had her own magical treat. Don't get me wrong. I wasn't trying to give these ladies cancer by feeding them sugar (if that's even possible). I felt anything, including sugar, is best when consumed in moderation and when it's shared among friends.

One day I didn't have time to individually wrap the treats so I popped a few truffles into a plastic bag then stuffed the bag into my purse. When I arrived in the treatment room, I explained to the peeps there was only one bag of goodies, and they would probably have to wrestle for it.

"Dana looks pretty buff so my money is on her," I taunted.

"Dana is tough, but there are two of us and one of her. We can gang up on her," Jennifer threatened. "In fact, she's going down, big time."

We all chuckled. I hugged Jennifer to show her I appreciated her humor.

"I feel like I could hug each of you every day, but that would probably be inappropriate," I shared.

"You can hug us as much as you want," Jennifer replied. "In fact, we probably need it."

The holiday treats were a great way to break the ice with the technicians each day. "What kind of goodies did you bring for us today?" they would ask before I had a chance to set the treats on the table. As the days turned into weeks, I began to build a relationship with each of the technicians. I learned about their likes and dislikes, their hobbies, and about their family and friends.

On one particular Friday, I entered the "Bat Cave" as I referred to the treatment room because it was dark and cold. I noticed that not only the physical atmosphere was gloomy, but the entire feel and tone of the room was one of melancholy. No one asked me what kind of treat I had brought, which was very uncharacteristic. So I volunteered the information.

"Girls, I have homemade fudge for you today," I announced.

"Sounds good," Jennifer replied in a monotone voice.

Sounds good was not the response I had expected. Homemade fudge was pretty high on the food chain hierarchy. It ranked second only after Rice Krispie treats. Something was up.

"I can tell you three aren't your regular perky selves. What's the matter?" I asked.

The three of them shot laser beam glances around the room at each other. I knew the look so well from the kids at recess. It was the "should I tell or not tell" look.

"Okay, we'll tell you, but we haven't told anyone else. We have a patient who comes in every morning who is so angry," Dana confessed.

"She's mean to us. Let's just say it like it is," Jennifer chimed in. "Today she was in rare form and really bit our heads off. It's bothered us all day."

83

"We understand why she is angry. It happens to many of our patients. They are angry about having cancer. They are asking themselves, 'Why did this happen to me?' All that anger gets bottled up inside, and many times it is taken out on us. We totally understand that," Rose added. "But our understanding of the situation doesn't make it hurt any less."

There was an extended length of silence in the room as I took the time to soak in what they had shared with me and to think about my response to them. It was the "think time" I had been training my students to use in order to develop thoughtful, intelligent, and reflective responses.

"First of all, thank goodness it is Friday. The weekend will give everyone the opportunity to think. She'll calm down. You three will calm down. Monday will roll around, and it will have a different tone to it. Agreed?" I began.

"That's true," they chimed in at different times.

"Second of all, you don't have to take that from a patient or from any human being. To earn respect, we all must treat each other with respect. What if you tell her how you feel? Start with something like, 'We understand dealing with cancer is frightening and scary, and the situation can make you angry. But it hurts our feelings when you lash out at us. We are here to help you. We are on your team. Can you work with us?' End with a question. Leave it open-ended. Put the ball in her court," I suggested.

This time there was extended silence on their part. Perhaps they needed a little "think time."

"We'll think about it," Rose said. "Let's get your treatment over with so we can all start our weekends."

"Sounds good," I agreed, echoing their initial words back to them.

They were back to their giggling selves, licking the fudge remnants off of their fingers when they returned from their lead encased room.

"We think there might be something magical about this fudge because it made us realize something," Dana began.

"We're glad you are our last patient we see every day," Jennifer chimed in. "You are always so positive. It's a great way for us to end each day, and in this case, it is a great way for us to start the weekend."

"Thank you for sharing that with me," I said. This was ironic I thought. That was exactly how I felt when my students sent me off each day. It's interesting how events in life come full circle. "I don't bring you treats every day to butter you up. I bring them as a simple token of my gratitude and appreciation for all you do for me. As for my positive attitude, it's just part of my 'radiant' personality. " As I said the word radiant, I made quotation marks with my fingers around my head hoping they would get the pun.

"Get dressed so you can take your 'radiant' personality home," chuckled Rose. "We'll see you on Monday."

Chapter 8
The Only Constant is Change

Before I became a teacher, I worked in the
business world as a buyer for an electronic
distribution company. I purchased semiconductors,
sockets, transistors, and motherboards from the
factories in California in large, bulk orders. Then
our company would sell these items in smaller
quantities to our customers. I quickly learned this
was a very fast paced and business. My boss at the
time summed it up with these words, "The only
constant in life is change."

Once my radiation treatments began, I had
settled into a structured routine, but there were
changes within that routine. One of the most
shocking changes occurred when I walked into the
radiation treatment waiting room one afternoon and
gazed upon Rosanna's bald head.

"What's up? No scarf today?" I asked as I sat
down beside her.

"You're not going to believe this! My hair is
growing back!" Rosanna squealed with excitement.

It is? I thought to myself. I couldn't see any
hair. Rosanna must have seen the puzzled look on
my face.

"Feel it! Just rub your hand across the top of my
head," she insisted as she angled her head toward
me.

I did as I was instructed. Sure enough, I could
feel a thin layer of fine hair, which reminded me of
the fuzz on a fresh peach. For some reason, I

thought Rosanna's hair would be more like the stubble of a man's beard when it grew back.

"That's amazing," I slowly whispered. "I'm so happy for you."

"I know. I am so ecstatic about having hair again. I can't even tell you with words! On the drive here, I rolled down all the car windows just so I could feel the wind blow through my hair," she explained. She must have been excited because it was the middle of December, which really wasn't "let the wind blow through your hair" kind of weather. We discussed possible styling options for her new hair, along with adding a few cute baseball caps to her headwear collection. Our conversation was interrupted when Rosanna's name was announced, and she was headed down the hall to her treatment session.

"I'll see you and your new hair tomorrow," I called after her.

She turned to wave at me, and that's when I noticed the huge smile on her face. It was amazing what a little "peach fuzz" could do. At times, as a cancer patient, you learn not to sweat the small stuff. At other times, you learn to appreciate the small stuff.

As the radiation was being put into my body on a daily basis, my energy was being zapped out. As the days turned into weeks, I went from being a little tired to being totally exhausted by the end of each day. It was a struggle to prepare the evening meal, let alone clean up the kitchen afterwards. I usually graded papers from seven until ten each night, but now by eight I was asleep on the couch with the papers strewn over me like a blanket. When Saturday rolled around, I barely had the energy to complete my weekly household chores.

I knew my energy level was only going to get worse as the radiation treatments continued. I knew something was going to have to change. I was reminded of the words of my former boss . . . the only constant in life is change.

I did just that. I changed things up a bit. I went through my cookbooks and did some research on-line, searching for recipes for crockpot meals. In the mornings when I had the most energy, I prepared the meals, putting the food in the crockpot and simply turning it on. When we arrived home each evening, the house had a heavenly, delicious smell, and all I had to do was put the food on our plates. Often on Fridays after I collected Landon from the bus stop, we would pick up a pizza on the way home so I didn't have to cook. Needless to say, Landon loved this new son/mom tradition.

Near the end of December, we had a two-week winter break from school, so I used that time to cook several meals and put them in the freezer to use once school started again. I also used that time to catch up on grading the students' work.

As for the housework, I decided if the furniture had a thin layer of dust and the carpets weren't vacuumed once a week, it was okay. I conserved what little energy I had to do the laundry and keep the kitchen and bathrooms clean. I just needed to decide what was important and what I needed to let slide.

I realized there were changes occurring in my routine, but I was also going through an emotional metamorphosis. A bit of self-pity was starting to sneak into my life. My tried and true cure for this ailment was a healthy dose of good deeds. It is hard to feel sorry for yourself when you are busy helping someone else.

God had planted an idea in my head when I went to purchase my aluminum free deodorant and special lotion to treat my skin throughout my radiation treatments. Purchasing the deodorant was not a problem. It was reasonably priced at the local grocery store. The lotion was a different story. As far as I knew, it could only be purchased at the hospital pharmacy for an exorbitant price and only after having your name on a waiting list for several weeks. I thought about all the things I needed to do in preparation for my radiation treatments. I had to get my "buff" tattoos, arrange for a substitute teacher to be in my classroom, arrange for Landon to be dropped off at the bus stop instead of riding home with me, and obtain the special deodorant and lotion. In addition to all this, I still needed to come to grips with the fact that I had been diagnosed with cancer and, even after treatment, there was always the possibility it would return.

I know I wasn't the only person who felt overwhelmed as they journeyed through this process. So I began to think of ways I could reduce the stress for other people who were going through the cancer battle. The simplest thing at the moment seemed to be to provide the deodorant and lotion. I knew I couldn't afford to purchase these items myself, but I knew there were other ways to obtain these products. All I needed to do was to put in some time, hard work, and add a little ingenuity.

An on-line search of the companies who made these products yielded addresses for these businesses. I quickly wrote and sent emails explaining my project. Tom's of Maine Natural Deodorant responded immediately with an email stating their company would be honored and excited to be part of this endeavor. They would donate as much deodorant as we needed and would be happy to pay for the shipping as well. I was encouraged by their response. Maybe this wasn't such a crazy idea after all.

The company that made the lotion was willing to sell the product to me at the wholesale rather than the retail price, and I would have to pay for the shipping. I wasn't discouraged about the response. In fact, I was excited that they had offered me a discount because as far as I was concerned the Elta Lite Lotion seemed to be liquid gold. All I had to do was come up with the money to pay for it, but God had planted an idea in my head and now that idea was growing. The answer to this new challenge was . . . the kids. I had wanted to involve not just the students in my class, but all the kids in the entire school. This was the opportunity to do exactly that.

I was one of the staff advisors for the student council. Each month, the student council planned a spirit day, which usually meant wearing school colors or your favorite sports team's t-shirt in exchange for a small fee of twenty-five to fifty cents. Then the student council donated the money that was collected to a different charity each month. We cleverly called it "change for charity."

I have to admit, I loved spirit days for many reasons. When everyone arrived at school wearing the same thing, it built a sense of community. There's something to be said about knowing you belong to a group, knowing there is something out there that's bigger than you. It makes you feel proud. Second, I believe kids need to be taught about charitable giving just as they are taught reading, math, writing, science, and history. There's something about helping other people that makes you a better person, one who knows about empathy and generosity. Third, I wanted the kids to learn about teamwork. I wanted them to realize, through a real life experience, what they could accomplish as a group could be greater than what they could accomplish as individuals. Finally, I wanted to raise awareness about cancer. I knew just like the kids in my class, the kids in the entire school had been touched by cancer, whether it was a family member, a neighbor, a friend, or a teacher who had been diagnosed. I wanted them to know that through our actions, we could do something about cancer. We could be victors rather than victims.

I shared all this with Joanna and Laura, the two other teachers who were also student council advisors. At the end of my presentation I asked if the next spirit day's funds could be donated to the purchase of the lotion. They agreed it was a good idea, so my next step was to present the project to the members of the student council. Of course this was student government, so the idea had to be voted on, and it passed with flying colors.

The deodorant was already being shipped from the east coast to my home in Colorado. With a yes vote from the student council, I decided to place the order for the lotion, sending a personal check, and hoping we would raise enough money to reimburse me.

With all these changes occurring, there was also Christmas to prepare for. Ah, Christmas. I couldn't forget about this joy-filled holiday. This Christmas was going to be like no other but not for the reasons I had anticipated.

Chapter 9
It's Beginning to Look A Lot Like Christmas

I must confess that I love Christmas, every aspect and detail about it. I realize this is true for many people, but in my case I could easily be classified as a Christmas fanatic. I decorate the house before the Thanksgiving leftovers are cold. I buy Christmas gifts throughout the year, stashing them in secret hiding places throughout our home. The piece de resistance of this affliction is that I listen to Christmas music all year long. Because of these behaviors, my son and daughter often refer to me as "weird" to which I reply "thank you."

"Why would I want to be like everyone else?" I would ask them. To them, this question only added to my "weirdness."

Although I admit to being a Christmas fanatic, there was someone who loved Christmas even more than I did . . . my sister, Barb. During the holidays her house looked like Christmas had exploded both on the inside and the outside of her home. She decorated every room, including the bathrooms. The exterior of her home . . . let's just say that the Griswold family from the "Christmas Vacation" movie had nothing on her.

During one of our Saturday phone calls, it was with great sorrow I had to break the news to Barb that we wouldn't be coming home for Christmas. Home was the small town in northern Iowa where I grew up and where Barb still lived. Greg, the kids, and I usually rotated spending Christmas in Iowa with my family one year then in western Colorado with Greg's family the next year. This year it was going to be neither of those two destinations. Christmas and New Year's Day were during the weekends so there were no days to be taken off from my radiation treatments. We had decided to celebrate a quiet, peaceful Christmas in the comfort of our own home.

Barb understood about the situation when I explained it to her, but I could tell by the tone of her voice she was a little disappointed. I desperately wanted to make it up to her. I reminded her that I would be home in May for a wedding, hoping that fact would be somewhat of a consolation prize. Then I thought of something even better.

Barb had asked me for many years to join her for the Relay for Life. It was the biggest fundraiser for the American Cancer Society in the area. She put countless hours into it. It truly was her pride and joy, her baby. Each summer we usually had a small vacation planned, or I was taking classes to renew my teaching certificate so unfortunately I rarely saw Barb in all of her well-earned glory at the Relay for Life.

"Remember three years ago when I came home, and we did the Relay for Life together?" I asked her. "I can't come back for it this summer since I will have just been home for the wedding in May, but how about next summer we do the Relay for Life not just as sisters but as survivors?"

"Are you serious?" she responded. "That would be great!"

"I am serious," I assured her. "This whole 'cancer thing' has helped me see life with a new perspective. I'm prioritizing things a little differently now."

"Yeah, cancer has a way of doing that to you," she offered.

"Hey Barb, there's one more thing I've got to tell you, not only about the Relay for Life, but the whole 'cancer thing' . . . we've got this. We can do this!" I attempted to cleverly use the same words she was always telling me.

"Yeah, you're right," she answered. "We can do this."

After my conversation with Barb, I continued to cruise through the holiday season crossing items off my to do list like a "mad woman." The house was decorated, inside and out. The gifts were purchased, wrapped, and waiting under the Christmas tree. I had made and delivered holiday goodies to all the neighbors. Of course, the Christmas music was blaring throughout our house and in my car.

Suddenly, I hit a speed bump on the road to a merry Christmas. What was I going to give Rosanna and my radiation peeps? I wanted to give them something but giving a gift viewed as extravagant would be inappropriate. I found my inspiration in one of my favorite quotes from Leonardo Da Vinci, "Simplicity is the ultimate form of sophistication."

Even though I made my living by being a teacher, I have always considered myself to be a writer. As a young girl, I was constantly writing poems, plays, stories and creating greeting cards. I have always felt that words, if used in the right way, can be gifts we give to each other. With that in mind, I bought a box of the most beautiful Christmas cards I could find. I sat down one evening with pen in hand and wrote heartfelt notes in the cards to Rosanna and each of my radiation peeps. I wrote my innermost thoughts regarding how each of these sweet ladies had helped me progress through my cancer journey and, in the process, how each of them had become my friend. Personally, I thought professing my gratitude, appreciation and friendship to them was an awesome gift. I hoped they would think so, too.

At this point, the Christmas cards had been delivered. I'd given gifts to my students and the staff at school. When Christmas morning finally arrived, it was time to exchange gifts with our family. Greg's mom had decided to join us for the holidays. It seemed strange when just the five of us gathered next to the Christmas tree. Usually we were surrounded by a mob of relatives who created a buzz of happy excitement in the room.

Landon and Sierra had each celebrated another birthday in the fall and were now twelve and sixteen years old. Anyone who has raised children knows it is a challenge to buy gifts for people who are these ages. They weren't little kids any more, but they weren't adults either. Each time they began to open a gift, Greg and I would tease them stating that a chia pet was lurking inside. Ah, those crazy chia pets, which are pottery shaped like a person or animal. Once water is added, the seeds inside the pottery sprout into plants and become the hair or fur of the person or animal. Much to their relief, none of the gift boxes actually contained chia pets. Most contained several articles of clothing and the coveted gifts cards from Amazon and I-tunes.

Finally, one lonely, small package was left under the branches of the tree. Greg picked it up and handed it to me. With a mischievous look on his face, he said, "This one is for you."

"You know how much I love surprises," I said as I began to rip off the wrapping paper. When the paper finally dropped to the floor, I was left holding what appeared to be a DVD case. Strangely enough, there wasn't a title on the cover, only a photo of a man and woman sitting on the grass of what seemed to be the lawn of a college campus.

I didn't want to appear ungrateful, and I did want to be sincere so I just asked, "What is this?"

"I'm taking you on a trip!"

"To where?"

"To anywhere in the world you want to go this summer when we both have a break from school. The DVD is from the travel agency I've been working with in town. It showcases the most popular destinations in the world."

"We're going on a trip!" Sierra screamed with excitement, and soon Landon chimed in with her.

"No, no, no. You two aren't going on a trip. Mom and I are going on a trip. You two are going to Grandma's," Greg calmly told the kids.

The "we're going on a trip" chant came to an abrupt halt. There was a moment of hesitation as the words Greg spoke sank in for all of us in the room. Sierra and Landon briefly looked at each other before beginning to chant, "We're going to Grandma's house. We're going to Grandma's house." Soon they were discussing all the activities Grandma would let them do that they weren't allowed to do at home.

"Grandma, will you let us drink coffee?" Landon asked Greg's Mom as he dramatically licked his lips. "And can we have ice cream sundaes every night?"

"Grandma, will you let me drive your car?" Sierra pondered out loud.

"We'll see," Grandma Inez responded with a chuckle.

"What do you think?" Greg asked me above the hum of the kids' conversation.

Granted, I do enjoy surprises, especially if I am the person surprising someone else, but there is a distinct difference between being surprised and being shocked. I was definitely the latter. I believed that two people who are public school teachers cannot afford to go on a trip to anywhere in the world.

I was thinking . . .*what in the world is Greg thinking?!?!* But I said, "I love it." I hugged his neck tightly and kissed his cheek.

It was a quiet, peaceful Christmas day. We consumed a turkey dinner with all of the fixings at about 2 p.m. Landon proclaimed it "linner," a combination of lunch and dinner. We grazed on leftovers the remainder of the afternoon and into the evening. At about 8 p.m. Greg, his mom, and the kids had settled in for a night of watching TV. I excused myself to the master bedroom stating I wanted to read the book Greg's mom had given me as a Christmas gift, but I really just wanted time to think.

I sat on the edge of the bed with the new book in my lap even though I had no intention of reading it at that moment in time. An image of the travel DVD Greg had given me flashed in my mind. Why had he given me a trip? Was he afraid I was going to die, and we would never have the chance to travel like we had always dreamed of?

Greg was no stranger to cancer. His father had died of brain cancer long before I met Greg. He knew about the process, the surgeries, the chemotherapy, radiation, and medications. Even though his father went through all of the recommended treatments, cancer still took his life while his son watched helplessly.

Greg's Christmas gift made me question myself. Had I been so busy taking care of other people that I had overlooked caring for my husband and children? I knew I had made the people in the school community feel comfortable. I knew I had kept them informed throughout the entire process, and I had continually assured them that their needs would be met. But had I done the same for my own family?

I have often said that the cancer journey is unique for each cancer patient. But the journey is also unique for each person who has a relationship with a cancer patient.

Landon's way of dealing with my cancer diagnosis was total denial. He didn't want to talk about it. End of story. As far as he was concerned, the only thing that had changed in life was that he rode the bus home every afternoon instead of riding with me.

Sierra, on the other hand, dealt with the situation with unbridled anger, which was directed at me. I wasn't sure if the cause of her emotions was my cancer diagnosis or the fact that she was a sixteen-year-old girl. Maybe it was a little of both.

I tried to look back to when I was sixteen in order to understand her feelings. At that age, I also had a parent who was a cancer patient, my dad. He had a cancerous lung removed. I don't remember feeling angry. I remember feeling afraid that I would no longer have him in my life. Ironically, even though I was the child, and he was the parent, I bustled about him like a mother hen. I reminded him to wear his mask when he went out into the cold, winter air. I suggested he keep a bandana in his pocket to use when he forgot his mask. Finally, when his patience wore thin, he lovingly told me to "lay off."

As I continued to struggle with understanding the reactions of my children and husband, I began to think of the cause of all this turmoil . . .cancer. When you battle cancer, it is imperative to understand the many weapons your opponent has in its arsenal. Cancer is not only elusive but ambiguous. Even though the word cancer is a noun, as a cancer patient, you can't really see it or touch it but know it's there. It reaches its sinister tentacles into every aspect of your life, your physical being, your financial stability, your relationships, your emotional well-being, and even your spirituality. I wanted so desperately to be able to reach out and grab cancer by the throat in order to choke the very life out of it. Maybe that's how my family felt as well. How can you fight something you can't see or touch? Then the proverbial light bulb went off inside my head. If we were battling something that couldn't be seen or touched, maybe our weapons needed to be things that couldn't be seen or touched. I think Landon and Sierra both needed time. Perhaps with time, Landon would be able to talk and share his feelings with me once we returned to our afternoon car pool situation with just the two of us traveling the rural roads to school and home. Perhaps with time, Sierra would emerge from her cocoon spun with anger and irritation as the beautiful butterfly I hoped she would become. Yes, time would be one of the weapons I would use against cancer, but you can't fight a battle with just one weapon. Love. Love could be my other weapon. You can't see or touch love, but we all know that you can't live without it. It is as essential as the invisible air we breathe. Love and time, these would be my weapons of choice.

By now my thoughts had come full circle back to Greg and his magnificent Christmas gift. Perhaps he had given me two more weapons to add to my arsenal . . . hope and faith. I was stuck in the realm of day to day living; going to work, having a radiation treatment, cooking, cleaning, sleeping, repeat. Greg's gift reminded me to look into the future because that is where hope lives; without hope we have nothing. Everyone deserves to dream, to look to the future and visualize what we think it will be like. Dreams and hope are what motivate us to keep going in search of what we think will be a better life, in search of happiness. These ideas seemed somewhat simplistic, but this was my truth. How would we pay for this trip to anywhere in the world? Well, that is where the faith part came into play. We would trust that God would provide. Hope and faith were now two new weapons I had to battle against cancer. How clever of Greg to disguise hope and faith in a travel DVD. At least a DVD was easier to giftwrap.

I rose from the edge of the bed, made my way downstairs, and snuck up behind the couch where Greg was sitting. I planted a big, wet kiss on the bald spot on the top of his head. Then I wrapped my arms around his neck, brushing my cheek against his. "I love the Christmas gift you gave me," I whispered into his ear, and this time I meant it.

Landon, Pam, and Sierra

Chapter 10
Change

Strange as it may sound, I kept having a reoccurring vision of myself in a boxing ring. Fortunately, in this vision, I am my slender self, like back in my college days. I'm wearing red, white, and blue, silk boxing shorts and a white sleeveless muscle shirt. From a distance, I can see my opponent seated in the corner of the ring, and I think it is Apollo Creed. In a defensive move, I raise my gloves up to protect my face, simultaneously keeping my elbows and arms at my sides to protect my abdomen. I am in the center of the ring. My opponent is approaching, but I still can't see him clearly, so I cautiously peer over my gloves. That's when it happens. BAM! A sucker punch to the face! When I finally recover from the shock and regain my vision, I realize it wasn't Apollo Creed who hit me, but Rocky Balboa. Crazy, right?

At first I struggled to find the meaning of this vision, but over time I came to the following conclusion. Before my brother Steve died of colon cancer at the age of forty-eight, I promised him that I would have a colonoscopy even though I was only thirty-eight. At that time, the recommended age to have an initial colonoscopy was fifty. Due to the history of colon cancer on my mother's side of the family, I had no problem convincing my doctor that it would be a good idea for me to undergo the procedure early.

I knew I was in that boxing ring with cancer, but I thought my opponent was colon cancer. I prepared myself accordingly by having my gloves on and maintaining a defensive stance . . . an early colonoscopy. When the test results came back clear, I let myself put my defenses down. I was okay for a while but then out of nowhere BAM! I was broadsided with breast cancer. I wasn't expecting it. No one in my family had ever been diagnosed with breast cancer. It was a shock to say the least.

My initial diagnosis was the sucker punch to the face. Paying for the surgery was a direct hit to the abdomen. One punch to the abdomen is uncommon. It's usually a combination of punches. The second punch arrived in the mail during the first week in January. It was the bill for my radiation treatments in December. The copay amount was staggering. Fortunately, I still had money in the emergency fund, but this would nearly drain it. It seemed so ironic that what had taken me years to save would be gone in an instant as soon as I signed the check and sent it off in the mail. Cancer may have smashed me in the face and given me the one/two punch to the gut, but I was determined I wasn't going down for the count. I would readjust my strategy and continue to fight.

Even though the radiation bill had knocked the wind out of me while I was struggling to regain my breath, I still thought of the positive. During Christmas break, I had managed to complete twelve radiation treatments without using any sick days. The break was ten days long. There was a workday

104

before the break and an in-service day before school started again in January. I could leave early on those two days and not be docked sick days. It was another example of looking for the up side of a situation.

Before any self pity could creep into my life, I jumped into the deodorant/lotion donation project. The deodorant had already been donated and shipped to my home. The plan was to use the money collected from the school's January spirit day to reimburse me for the lotion.

The kids at school were always jazzed about school spirit days, but they especially enjoyed our January pajama day. I think they loved just rolling out of bed and coming to school without putting on regular clothes.

"At least brush your teeth and comb your hair," I always told them the day before.

The student council members were on fire making banners and posters for the upcoming spirit day. We had put an article in the school newsletter describing the event and how we would use the money we collected. Everyone was pumped with anticipation.

Finally, the day of the event arrived. The adrenaline was flowing as I stood in the hall just outside of my classroom door as I did every morning. Only on this day I was dressed in my fuzzy, mint green, hooded robe wearing moccasin bedroom slippers. I felt like I was cheating a little bit because I had my regular clothes on underneath. Fortunately, the kids never found out.

The usual protocol for a spirit day was for the classroom teachers to collect the change from their students in plastic food storage bags. Student council representatives would then collect the bags from the classrooms and deliver them to the sixth grade rooms where the student council members and officers would count the money.

It was clear as soon as the first bell rang that it was going to be a day for protocols to be thrown out of the window. As I stood in the hall waiting for my daily high fives, fist bumps, and hugs, I quickly realized there were added components to this morning's usual greetings . . . bags of money.

One of the students from my class proudly held up a clear, plastic bag bulging with coins.

"This is for you, Mrs. Pottorff!" he exclaimed.

I was stunned but calmly replied, "Where did you get all of that money?"

"I asked my parents if I could have any money I found around our house. They agreed. I didn't find much under the cushions of the sofa and chairs. Then I hit the jackpot!" he explained. "There was a ton of money in the cup holders of my parents' cars!"

"Wow! That was very creative thinking on your part," I complimented him as he handed me the bag of coins and sauntered into the classroom wearing his Bugs Bunny slippers.

An older student was next. She carefully handed me a white envelope as if it were the results of the Miss Universe pageant.

"Open it, Mrs. Pottorff," she instructed.

I opened the envelope as carefully as she had handed it to me. Inside was a check for a fairly large amount of money. I looked up from the check with a look of disbelief plastered across my face.

"We had a family meeting last night, and we decided this is how much money we wanted to donate," she happily explained as a huge smile spread across her face.

I was speechless. This level of giving was so unexpected. I simply reached out and gave her a hug, then whispered, "Thank you."

"You're welcome!" she replied in a perky, sunshine-filled voice as she skipped down the hall to her classroom in her onesie pajamas.

There was a tug on my robe. It was one of the second graders who often followed me around at lunch recess. He was one of those kids who interacted better with adults than he did with his peers. I'd let him converse with me for half of the recess, then we had an agreement that he needed to play with the other kids for the second half of recess. Through our recess conversations, we had built a lovely, comfortable relationship.

"Here, Mrs. Pottorff. I know I am supposed to turn this in at my classroom, but I wanted to give this to you in person," he said as he handed me a twenty-dollar bill enclosed in a clear, plastic bag.

"You know you only have to bring change to wear your pajamas today, right?" I explained.

"I know, but I wanted to donate this," he countered.

"Where did you get this money?" I asked. "It's so crisp and new."

"It's my birthday money," he said.

I felt a lump forming in my throat, and I knew tears were welling up in my eyes. I couldn't take a kid's birthday money. That would be like the scoundrels who scam senior citizens out of their life's savings over the phone. It was lower than low.

"I can't take your birthday money," I explained. "You just wear your pajamas today and put this money in your backpack to take home tonight."

"No, Mrs. Pottorff. You don't understand," he said in a shaky, emotional voice. "I called my Grandma and told her what I wanted to do with the money she gave me for my birthday. She said she was proud of me for giving it to people who really needed it. She said it was a sign that I was growing up. I don't want her to be disappointed in me. Please take the money and help people who have cancer. Besides, giving the money makes me (he paused for several seconds)
...feel happy." Then a smile spread across his face. I took the money, hugged him, and told him thank you.

"Tell your Grandma thank you, too," I told him as he turned to go to his classroom. I watched him toddle down the hall in his Spiderman pajamas. Today he was dressed like a superhero, but in my world he was a superhero! Suddenly, he turned around as if he had forgotten something.

"See you at recess," he yelled down the hall.

"See you at recess," I yelled back, only this time I was the one with the shaky, emotional voice.

I know many of the students wanted to personally give me their donations in the hall that morning, and I could totally understand why. The situation was similar to how I felt about battling cancer. I wanted desperately to grab cancer and throw it as far away from humanity as I could. Much to my frustration, I couldn't because cancer seemed to be an elusive, invisible foe.

The kids knew we were going to use the money collected to purchase lotion for cancer patients but they didn't know those people. Yet, here I was standing in the hall as if I were a representative of all those people we were intending to help. I was someone they could see, touch, hug, and interact with, so they came to me with outstretched arms holding bags of change. I saw those outstretched arms as a symbol of our school community saying, "We want to help." We want to help people we don't even know. Isn't that what humanity is all about? Yes, we were learning lessons, lessons that weren't found in books or on websites, but lessons that would change our lives and the lives of others forever.

The second bell rang, awakening me from my joy-filled trance. I instructed the remaining students to turn their money in at their classrooms and sent them off down the halls with fist bumps, high fives, and hugs. Then I scurried into my classroom to take lunch count and attendance.

At about eleven o'clock, two sixth graders appeared at our classroom door holding gallon Zip Lock bags filled with coins and paper money.

"Mrs. Pottorff, you are not going to believe how much money we have collected!" one of the sixth grade students shared.

"It's the most money we've ever collected for a spirit day!" the other one added.

Again I was shocked and speechless. "That's amazing," I stammered. "You two need to take it to the office. Ask if you can announce the total over the intercom."

"That's what our teachers told us to do, but we wanted to stop and tell you the good news!"

"I'm glad you did," I shared as I gave each student a hug and sent them off to the office.

A few moments later we heard their voices on the intercom. They did an excellent job making the announcement have a dramatic flare.

"Attention Larkspur Bobcats," their voices blared through the hallways. "We would like to tell you the amount we have collected today during spirit day. It is actually a spirit day record! We collected (there was a long pause) $793!"

A collective cheer, much like the roar of a pride of lions, echoed throughout the entire school building. I was so overwhelmed I had to sit down on the stool in the front of the room.

"Are you okay, Mrs. Pottorff?" a student asked.

"I'm more than okay," I answered.

Cancer had bashed me in the face and given me the one/two punch to the gut, but I wasn't going down. I was on a journey, and today it was clear I wasn't on that journey alone. As I traveled, I was changing and so were my fellow travelers. Today the entire student body had learned several priceless lessons. They had learned about the joy and ecstasy of generosity and empathy, about thinking of others before yourself. They had learned how empowering it is to realize how much you can accomplish together rather than alone. I had to chuckle because ironically, we had all learned such deep, life-changing, enduring lessons on a day when everyone was dressed in their pajamas. How silly was that?

As I sat in the front of my class dressed in my fuzzy, hooded robe and moccasin slippers, I realized this journey we were on was changing all of us for the better. *BAM, cancer! Here's a sucker punch to your face!*

Chapter 11
The House That Love Built

The remainder of the day seemed normal, other than the fact that the entire school population was wearing pajamas. At 2 p.m., a student carried my backpack to my car as usual. I rewarded him with a Jolly Rancher candy then patiently waited for him to disappear into the school before I removed my robe and slippers.

I didn't listen to my usual classic rock music on my drive to the cancer center because I needed time to think about the events of the day. I had already made a sizeable donation towards the purchase of the lotion, so initially I asked the student council to cover the remainder of the bill, which was $150. That day we had miraculously raised $793. I still couldn't believe it! That meant we had $643 to help even more cancer patients. At this moment in time, I wasn't certain what that help would look like. One thing I was certain about was God would show me how the funds were to be used.

When I entered the treatment room that day, I explained the situation to my radiation peeps and asked them for their input.

"What about 'The House That Love Built'?" suggested Jennifer.

"That's a great idea," Dana added.

"What is 'The House That Love Built'?'" I asked.

"It's like a Ronald McDonald House where cancer patients and their families can stay for free while the patient receives care here at the cancer center," Rose explained. "The official name of the place is The John Zay Guesthouse, but everyone around here calls it 'The House That Love Built,' because it was built totally through donated materials and volunteer hours."

After the completion of my radiation treatment, the peeps returned from their lead encased room still munching the banana bread I had brought for them.

"I can't thank you enough for the suggestion about 'The House That Love Built'," I told them as I dressed behind the screen.

"Why don't you drive by it on your way home?" Rose suggested. "It's basically right across the street from here." Then she gave me quick directions. It was Friday, and I knew the peeps were anxious to go home to start their weekends. I gave them each a big bear hug as a form of my appreciation before scurrying out of the door. I realized God had once again revealed His will to me through the voices of others.

When I drove up to the John Zay Guesthouse, my heart was pounding wildly in anticipation. The house seemed to have a magical, golden orb surrounding it. Perhaps it was just my imagination or perhaps it was a sign from God. I like to think it was the latter.

I parked my car and walked up to the inviting front porch with its majestic white pillars. No one came to the door after I had pushed the doorbell several times, so I tried turning the doorknob. My efforts proved that the door was locked, and no one was currently inside the elegant building. I returned to my car disheartened but definitely not discouraged.

Over the weekend, an online search uncovered a plethora of information about John Zay and the guesthouse. John Zay was a minister who was diagnosed with cancer. His cancer journey led him to minister to other cancer patients at the Penrose Hospital, which was where the current Rocky Mountain Cancer Center was housed. He ministered to cancer patients there for over fourteen years, and this eventually led to the idea of building a guesthouse for people who didn't live in the area but came to the cancer center for treatment. Although John Zay died in 2004, his legacy lived on through the guesthouse, which was named after him.

Throughout the entire weekend, I thought about Mr. Zay's life. I couldn't help but think he had been called by God to help cancer patients. I, too, felt called by God to help others traveling the cancer journey. Granted, my calling wasn't as grand as Mr. Zay's, but it was a calling just the same. Throughout my journey, I had learned to be aware of the many ways God had spoken to me. It wasn't like in the movies when a majestic, male voice speaks from luminous, parting clouds in the sky. Instead, I often experienced an aching feeling in my gut or wonderful ideas would suddenly pop into my head. At other times, fabulous visions would appear in my imagination like colorful videos. Sometimes events would happen unexpectedly. People often refer to these events as unusual circumstances, but I prefer the term happy accidents. I was convinced these were all examples of God's communication with me, and I was determined to pay attention to His messages.

The deodorants and lotions had already been shipped to my home. I decided to package the products myself rather than haul them to and from school in order to have the students do it. I had purchased several spools of hot pink ribbon, which I used to tie around one deodorant and one tube of lotion to create a bundle. I added a letter that briefly explained my cancer journey and the journey of my fellow travelers, the students who had raised the money to purchase the products. I also invited the recipients to reach out to the students by sending a letter or email to the school. The letters were carefully rolled into scrolls and tucked into the center of each bundle. When I finished, there were fifty bundles of deodorant, lotion, and letters wrapped with beautiful pink ribbons sitting on my dining room table. It was a wonderful sight to behold, so I took a photo to capture the moment. The photo turned out to be very useful. I shared it with the kids in my class and the members of student council. I also slipped copies of the photo into the handwritten thank you cards I sent to the makers of Tom's of Maine Deodorant and Eltra Lite Lotion. The next task on my to do list was to find a way to distribute the gift bundles.

Deodorant and Lotion Bundles

There have been many times in my life when I have had to swallow my pride, and I always find that it leaves a bitter aftertaste. Such was the case as I sat at my computer composing an email to the nurse navigator who had been assigned to my case. I had not had any contact with her since the first day I met her at which time she told me I "needed to act like I had cancer." Her comment had angered me, but I had decided to push that anger aside in order to ask her if she could be the person to distribute our deodorant/lotion bundles to people who had recently been diagnosed with cancer and were facing radiation treatments.

After several days, she responded to my email stating she would be happy to be part of the project. I arranged a time before one of my radiation treatments to drop off the products to her. Ironically, we never received even one response from any of the recipients, but that wasn't our goal. Our goal was to let people know that they weren't alone on their cancer journeys. We cared enough about them to give them a gift, which would help take care of a few of their physical needs. Even without any feedback from the recipients, the students and I still felt the project was a success.

At the next student council meeting, I not only shared the photo of the gift bundles, I also presented the idea of donating the remaining $643 from spirit day to the John Zay Guesthouse. The kids were all familiar with the concept of Ronald McDonald houses so when I explained the John Zay Guest House was similar, they loved the idea. The motion to donate the remaining money to "The House That Love Built" passed by a unanimous vote. I called the John Zay Guesthouse later that day to arrange a date and time when I could deliver the check.

My husband had voiced an interest in going with me to deliver the donation and to see what the guesthouse looked like, so I set the appointment for a Saturday afternoon. When we drove up to the guesthouse, Greg was just as impressed with the structure as I had been the first time I saw it.

The House That Love Built

117

This time when I pushed the doorbell, someone responded immediately. A friendly, middle-aged woman invited us in and informed us she would be giving us a tour of the main floor. The second floor consisted of the suites for the families, so out of respect for their privacy, tours never ventured to that part of the house.

The inside of the home was even more spectacular than the exterior. One room was clearly meant for families to gather and spend time together. The massive fireplace with its elegant molded mantle seemed to be the focal point. Wing back chairs and a large sofa covered with classic tapestries completed the sophisticated look of the room. The details of the room were the clues to its purpose. There was a partially completed puzzle on a table. Books and magazines were strategically placed around the room along with board games, stuffed animals, and lap blankets. This was clearly the place where families came to relax and hang out.

Another room contained a large TV and comfy furniture. Our next stop was the formal dining room with a table that could easily accommodate the Waltons, Brady bunch, or any large family. Our tour guide shared with us that the dining room was rarely used because the families liked to eat in the kitchen where the atmosphere was a bit more casual. When we reached the kitchen, it was clear to see that it was the epicenter of the home. The oversized appliances and immaculate appearance gave the room a commercial feel, but the large wall calendar and message board gave it a homey vibe.

Our tour guide proudly explained that several nights a week groups from the community came to cook for the guest house residents. On this particular night a group of students from a local Catholic High School would be preparing an Italian themed meal complete with spaghetti, meatballs, salad, rolls, and a dessert, which was going to be a special surprise. At that point, I asked where the families were today since the house appeared to be deserted. Our tour guide explained usually on Saturdays the families liked to visit many of the tourist attractions in the area, but they would be back in time to enjoy the special meal that was going to be prepared for them.

For the conclusion of the tour, our guide pointed out several items, which were unique to the guesthouse. The first was a beautiful pencil sketch of John Zay wearing a casual shirt and a baseball cap. The artist had done an excellent job in capturing his inviting smile and the twinkle in his eyes. The next precious item was a gorgeous curio cabinet filled with gifts and treasures given by grateful families who had temporarily made the house their home. Finally, there were two gigantic framed maps, one of the United States and one of the world. Small pushpins with heads of a variety of colors dotted both maps indicating where each family who stayed at the guesthouse lived. I was surprised to learn that families came from all over the world to be treated at the Rocky Mountain Cancer Center. That fact made me feel comforted and confident that I was receiving the best possible care.

We ended the tour in the room with the fireplace. As we sat on the elegant sofa, I presented the friendly tour guide with the check. She graciously accepted it explaining the money would probably be used to help pay for the utilities.

With our mission complete, my husband and I chatted briefly with our guide then left the guesthouse with our hearts and minds filled with gratitude, appreciation, and love. Truly, it was 'The House That Love Built," but I couldn't help thinking perhaps it was also 'The House That God Built' through His message to others to help one another.

When Monday morning rolled around, I eagerly shared our adventures and photos of the guesthouse with the kids in my class. They were very proud that their donations had gone to such a worthy cause. I also shared the information with my radiation peeps. They were proud they had played a part in the endeavor as well. Life seemed to be cruising along at an even keel until the next day, Tuesday, January 10th.

I walked into the radiation waiting room shocked to find Rosanna sitting in her regular chair with a full head of shoulder length dark brown hair!

"You've got to tell me what shampoo and conditioner you use to grow that much hair overnight," I said to her.

"Ha, ha, very funny," she replied.

"You never told me you had a wig," I said.

"It's one from the wig room they have by the main waiting room," she explained. "Are you familiar with that place?"

"Yes, I've seen a glimpse of it," I answered.

"I never wear it because it makes my scalp itch," she told me as she reached up to scratch her scalp making the entire wig move in a ridiculous motion across her head. We both laughed. "I decided to wear it today because it's my birthday, and I had to go get my driver's license renewed. I didn't want a picture of me with a bald head on my license for the next five years so I decided to wear my wig."

"Good choice," I told her. "You look fabulous, darling," I said in my most upscale accent. "Why didn't you tell me it was your birthday?"

"You know as well as I do that after a certain age women just want to stop having birthdays," Rosanna explained.

"I don't think it's the birthday that bothers women, but the number representing their age. It all goes back to our society's obsession with youth," I told her. "But after living through this whole cancer thing, I think I have a whole new perspective about birthdays. I'm going to cherish my next birthday and every birthday from now on.

"You're right. We should feel lucky and blessed to be able to celebrate another birthday," she agreed. "Speaking of celebrations, you know it won't be long until the two of us will be ringing the bell down the hall to celebrate our last radiation treatment."

"What bell are you talking about?" I asked.

"You're kidding me, right?" she chuckled. She glanced at me realizing by the look on my face that I wasn't kidding. "The bell down the hall on the way to the treatment rooms. You walk by it every single day. Come with me." We rose from our chairs, and I followed her down the corridor.

There on the wall in all of its glory was a shiny, gold bell about the size of a person's head attached to a wooden plaque. The words on the plaque read,

Ring this bell
Three times well,
The toll to clearly say . . .
My treatments done,
This course is run,
And I am on my way!

"I'm going to be ringing this bell in exactly one week from today!" Rosanna shared. "I can't wait."

I just stood there dumbfounded. How could I have walked by this every day and not noticed it? Why hadn't I heard or seen someone ring it?

The bell outside the treatment rooms triggered a vision of the school's bell tower on the playing field. It was very clear the vision was a message from God as to what he wanted me to do next. I had done everything He had asked me to do up until this point. I just didn't know if I had the courage, charisma, or self-confidence to do what He was asking me to do now.

Chapter 12
The Undeniable Voice of God

Rosanna's shoulder length hair was gone the next day. It was replaced by her beautiful spiked hair. I brought her a birthday card with a Starbuck's gift card slipped inside. She told me about her birthday activities, and we vowed once again never to take another birthday for granted.

"Let's do a countdown to your last treatment day," I suggested. "Are you in?"

"Yeah, sure. I like that idea," she answered. "I can't wait for that day!"

I knew that was true. Rosanna's cancer journey had been much longer than mine. She had taken the route of surgery with a round of chemotherapy followed by radiation treatments. If anyone deserved a countdown celebration, it was Rosanna.

"Great!" I said to her. "Six days and counting."

"Six days and counting is music to my ears," she added as she held her hand up inviting me to give her a high five.

Rosanna seemed to be on the right path in terms of reaching the end of her cancer journey. I, on the other hand, had reached a fork in the road and was unsure which path I should take. Would I select the uncertain yet beautiful path with the rough terrain God wanted me to take or the well-traveled, safe path my heart wanted me to select?

When Rosanna had shown me the bell in the hall that patients ring on their last treatment day, my mind immediately thought of the bell in the tower at school. It was a tradition to ring the bell on the first day of school each year to signify starting a new year with fresh ideas, dreams, wishes, and plans. I thought of the bell at the cancer center in the same way. Ringing it signified starting your life over as a cancer-free person who has a whole new perspective on life.

It has often been said that every journey has an end. Ringing the bell would bring closure to my cancer journey, but I realized I hadn't been on that journey alone. What would be the closure for the students, the staff, and community members at school? Didn't they deserve closure as well?

These were the questions God had planted in my mind that had made me realize I had reached a fork in the road on my journey. Not only had He planted these questions, but there was also a vision that kept repeating in my imagination like a video that was stuck on replay. The vision was an all school assembly celebrating my last treatment day and ending with the ringing of the bell in the tower.

I could see the power in His plan. Every teacher knows the power of review. It melds the bits and pieces of data from a lesson or unit into cohesive, meaningful, life long knowledge. When I looked back at the events of the past few months, I realized I had learned so much. As a teacher, my journey had been the greatest lesson I would ever teach. The lesson was about life. I had talked to third graders about mortality. As a school community, we had explored questions regarding our purposes in life. Do we live for ourselves, or do we enrich our lives by helping others? In a world so focused on "me", we had explored the concept of "us." We had learned we could accomplish so much more by working as a team rather than individuals.

So often in the school setting, we are focused on report cards, grades, percentages, and test scores. We reduce people to mere numbers for the sake of statistics. In doing so, we focus on the breadth of life. Because of my cancer diagnosis we were given a window of time to be able to focus on the depth of life. We asked ourselves pertinent questions, which had the capability of changing our lives. What is our purpose in life? How do we choose to spend our time? On what do we base our decisions? Who do we love and care about? How do we show love and compassion? What is empathy, and do we really need it? None of these questions or concepts will ever be found on a test, yet these ideas are just as important. Aren't these concepts what really make life worth living? Hopefully through our quest to find the answers to these questions, we all changed. We all became better people. Wasn't that worth celebrating? That was all God was asking me to do, to celebrate our journey and to bring closure to it, but it wasn't that simple, at least not for me.

I am not a person who draws attention to myself. I was the person who didn't want to wear her "Fight Like a Girl" shirt in public, and now God was asking me to orchestrate an assembly in front of hundreds of people. I didn't think I had what it would take to accomplish such a task. I was afraid. I was afraid of wasting people's time. I was afraid the assembly wouldn't be meaningful to anyone but me. I was afraid of looking like a fool. I was afraid of failure.

The first time God asked me to take on this endeavor when I was in the hall with Rosanna, I said no. I just wanted to take the easy path, to ring the bell at the cancer center on my last treatment day and be done with it.

I've learned many lessons in my life, and one of them has been that God is persistent. This situation was no different. Each day of the following week, visions of the assembly would pop into my mind along with an aching feeling in my gut. Each morning before school, I saw the vision as I sat at my computer checking my emails. During planning periods while I sat at the reading table grading papers, I heard God's voice whispering in my head. As I prepared the evening meals for my family, the aching in my gut intensified, and it wasn't because I was hungry. Each time these incidents occurred, I said no to God's request. All I knew was that I was afraid. Finally, on Friday night before I fell asleep, I gave in and said yes.

"I will do Your will," I told God. "But please help me and know that I am afraid."

Saturday morning I grabbed a spiral notebook and began scribbling notes from the visions I have been experiencing for the past week. By Sunday evening, the notes had morphed into a fine tuned outline for the assembly. A quick email to the school principal assured me a meeting time with him on Monday morning to propose the assembly and share the outline.

By the time Monday morning arrived, I was a nervous wreck. I knew convincing the principal would be no easy task. When I first began teaching

126

at the school, we had an assembly every Friday morning. I thought it was a fabulous tradition and such a marvelous way to build community. As the years progressed, "the powers that be" had decided the assemblies were not academically relevant and wanted to abolish them altogether. Due to the persistence of a few persuasive parents, we were allowed to have an assembly once a month. Knowing all this, I nervously stepped into the principal's office to plead my case. Fortunately, I knew I had God on my side. If I just opened my mouth, God would let the right words flow out. That is exactly what happened. The conversation ended with the principal giving me permission to hold the assembly on the morning of Tuesday, January 24th, the day of my last radiation treatment. There was a stipulation . . . the assembly could only last twenty minutes. *Maybe thirty*, the voice in my head whispered as I smiled and left the office.

That day after the bell had rung signaling the end of lunch recess, I let Joy take the class in so I could stay out on the playground. As I stood on the blacktop, I looked up the hill at the kickball diamond, replaying the game in which I kept kicking ground balls to third base allowing me the time to run to first. I strolled over to the foursquare courts and stood in the center of one. I remembered the games I played with the kids when I carefully hit the ball in the vacated sections of their squares. Finally, I walked to the section of the playground where the jump rope kids hung out. I recalled asking the girls to help me jump in as the rope was twirling. It took three times to jump in without the rope hitting me, but I made it, and I learned from my mistakes.

In each of these situations, I was trying something I hadn't done in years, and I was afraid of failing. But I had met that fear with strategies, and somehow knowing I had a plan had given me the confidence I needed.

I closed my eyes and remembered the day I had experienced the anxiety attack on the trial run for my radiation treatments. I was afraid on that day, too, but what carried me through the situation was the fact that I knew God was right there beside me. We never go through life's challenges alone. God is always with us, but it is so easy to lose sight of that fact.

"Help me, Lord. I am afraid," I confessed. Then all the pieces came together. I realized I had a strategy and had carefully planned out the assembly in great detail. I also had God, my all-knowing, loving, caring Father on my side.

With my eyes still closed, I lifted my face to the sun allowing its beams to warm my skin. A crisp Colorado breeze blew across my face as I realized my prayers had been answered. A voice whispered in my imagination, but it wasn't the booming male voice of God. It was a female voice I had heard throughout my entire life. It was my sister, Barb. "You can do this," she whispered. "You can do this."

Chapter 13
Angels Among Us

There was an older gentleman in the waiting room each day, but I rarely had the opportunity to speak with him. When I arrived he was already in a treatment room or just going in for his treatment. He came with a younger man who I assumed was his driver, but later I found out was his son.

Mid January, a man in his early forties walked into the waiting room. His bald head and thin frame indicated he was a cancer patient here for his radiation treatments. He seemed nervous and anxious. Everyone in the room knew exactly how he felt. In an effort to ease the tenstion, the older gentleman asked the "newbie" a simple question.

"How are you doing today?"

"I am fine," the younger man answered.

"You're not fine if you are here," the older man chuckled in a gravelly voice.

The Rosanna and I laughed because he was absolutely right. We were all cancer patients. None of us were "fine."

Before the younger man could respond, one of the technicians called the older man's name and proceeded to roll him down the hall in his wheelchair. His son took this as an opportunity to speak to all of us.

"Today is Dad's last treatment day," he began. " He's been through a lot. In April, he had a large section of his colon removed. He suffered a stroke on the operating table. After several months of rehab, he began chemotherapy and now he is just finishing up his radiation treatments today."

"Wow! He has been through so much. I had no idea," I said. "He always seems to have such a good attitude."

"He's always been that way," the son added. "In fact, he likes coming here each day. It gives him something to do. Otherwise he would just be sitting alone in his room at the care center. He is actually going to miss coming here every day."

Our conversation was interrupted because my name was called to receive my treatment. Seven minutes later, I emerged from the Bat Cave (treatment room) into the lighted hallway. Before me was the older gentleman standing near his wheelchair ringing the bell . . . alone. I had no idea where his son was. None of the technicians or nurses were around. He was there alone. It seemed to be a bittersweet moment. The positive was that he was ending his long string of cancer treatments. The negative was that now he had nowhere to go and no one to talk to each afternoon.

"Congratulations, you made it," I said as I walked up beside him.

"Yep, it has been a long time coming," he told me. "You day will happen soon." he added as he winked at me.

"Dad, did you ring the bell without me?" his son asked as he appeared from an adjacent hallway. "I just left to use the restroom."

"I couldn't wait," the older gentleman confessed. "I could ring it again if you want me to."

"Go for it," I added. "Nobody is around, and you've earned it." As I headed to the exit, I heard the sound of the bell echo through the hall. Let's just say the sounds suggested it was more than the allotted three clangs.

On the drive home, I thought of Rosanna. Her last treatment was only a few days away. I didn't want her to be alone for her bell ringing ceremony. I vowed I would speak to the peeps the next day to see if I could delay my treatment on the day Rosanna would ring the bell. That way I could celebrate with her. In fact, I decided to ask the peeps if they would join us in the hall. I wanted Rosanna's bell ringing ceremony to be more than a ritual. I wanted it to be a celebration.

That evening I was struggling with going to sleep because the events of the day kept replaying in my mind. No one should have to face cancer alone. After all there is strength in numbers. I reached over and touched Greg's shoulder.

"Greg, will you go with me on my last treatment day?" I asked.

"I've already planned on it, and the kids are coming, too," he replied.

Greg was always very proactive and in this case, very thoughtful. Cancer had touched my life but also the lives of everyone in our family. We should all celebrate the victory with the ringing of the bell. Finally, I had come to grips with the events of the day, so I peacefully snuggled into my pillow and drifted off to sleep.

Tuesday, January 17th was a red-letter day. It was Rosanna's last radiation treatment. When I entered the waiting room, Rosanna was sitting in her usual spot thumbing through a magazine. It was reminiscent of the first day I had met her. Only this time she wasn't wearing a yellow silk scarf around her head. She wasn't wearing her sporty, stylish wig either. That day she was proudly flaunting her beautifully spiked hair. Hair she cherished. Hair that had become her badge of courage and honor. Hair that she had earned. I plopped down in the chair beside her like I did every day.

"Are you excited?" I asked.

"Yes, and a little nervous."

"Why are you nervous?"

"It's weird and unexpected, but I've been doing treatments for so long and for every single day. I don't know what it's going to be like without it."

"I don't think it will take long for things to get back to normal for you. Whatever 'normal' is. One thing for sure, I'm really going to miss you."

"I'll miss you, too," she added. Our brief hug was interrupted by a technician calling Rosanna's name.

"See you in a few minutes," I told her. I stayed in the waiting room with my hands folded on my lap. For some unknown reason, now I was the one who was nervous. Time for prayer, I told myself. That was my go to strategy when I was nervous, apprehensive, anxious, or scared. Prayer was my go to strategy for everything.

Before I knew it, Rosanna was standing in the hall outside of the treatment room. I joined the radiation technicians who had gathered around her.

"Ready?" I questioned.

"Ready!" she answered as she grabbed the leather strap from inside the bell.

The first ring was a little weak, but she made up for it on the second. The third clang of the bell was out of this world! All of Rosanna's anger toward the dreaded disease known as cancer traveled through her body and into the bell. The sound of metal against metal echoed through the hallway announcing Rosanna's freedom to the world. She was free from daily treatments, free from chemo, free from surgery! At this moment in time, she was cancer free! The ringing of the bell was not only a celebration but also a declaration of starting life over with a whole new outlook.

Rosanna and I glanced at each other, smiled, then embraced.

"I won't see you tomorrow," I said as she turned to walk towards the exit. As I watched her walk down the corridor, I thought of my brother Steve's favorite song "Angels Among Us" sung by the country group Alabama. Throughout his cancer battle, he believed God sent people, a.k.a. angels, to help him through the toughest parts.

There goes my angel I thought as Rosanna disappeared from sight. Little did I know that I would never see that lovely lady again. We had exchanged phone numbers. Over the next few months I tried several times to contact her but received no response. I understand that people continually enter and leave our lives for a reason. The length of the friendship Rosanna and I shared didn't take away from the depth of it. Rosanna had appeared in my life just when I needed her the most to guide me through the radiation process and to become my trusted friend. Steve was right. There really are angels among us.

Chapter 14
The Ripple Effect

I wanted to wear something special for my last treatment day, and there was no doubt in my mind what that special something would be . . . the fight like a girl t-shirt Barb had given me. The shirt I had once been hesitant to wear now had become my badge of honor. I slipped a hot pink fleece jacket over it because it was always cold in our classroom. The watch with the pink wristband Barb had given me completed my ensemble.

When I arrived at school that morning, I set up the classroom as usual. I had just finished when I heard a knock at the outside door. A quick glance revealed the mother of one of my former students. Her face was pressed against the glass making her facial features look deformed.

I laughed as I let her in and continued to laugh when she said, "Sorry, you might have to wash that window."

It wasn't uncommon for parents to knock on my outside door in the mornings. Many of them were my friends, and sometimes that was the only opportunity we had to talk. I was grateful this mom had stopped by to visit for a few minutes. Our conversation took my mind off the assembly. Before I knew it, the bell rang, and the students drifted into the room to begin their morning seatwork. Strangely enough, some of them insisted on leaving their coats on stating the classroom was unusually cold. I didn't think anything of their requests because I had left on my hot pink fleece jacket for the same reason. Instead of focusing on their choice in clothing, I decided to focus on their behavior. I was proud of them for being so independent, but also a little disappointed that I didn't get to greet everyone in the hall like I usually did. Later, I would find out the events of that morning had all been carefully planned.

The morning routine went smoothly, and soon we were headed to the all-purpose room (gym, cafeteria, auditorium all rolled into one). As we walked down the hall, I could feel my body anticipating the assembly. My heart was pounding in my chest, and my palms were sweaty. I tried to calm myself by remembering that I had a plan, and God was right by my side. As I walked into the all-purpose room, I realized God was not only right there with me, but so were hundreds of other people who filled the room, and they were all dressed in pink.

I was shocked. I clutched my right hand to my chest, gasped for a breath, and fought back the tears. The class and I headed to our regular assembly spot, and quickly sat on the polished floor. The principal lead everyone in saying the Pledge of Allegiance before introducing me. My heart seemed to be exploding from my chest as I walked to the front of the room.

"Before we begin, we need to celebrate someone who is having a birthday today," I began. "Our own Mrs. Banister, otherwise known as Queen B, is celebrating a birthday today, so let's all sing happy birthday to her."

Kathy Banister was one of our fifth grade teachers and a dear friend of mine. While I was known as "The Supreme Empress" at school, she was known as "Queen B." It really was her birthday, and I knew I could count on her to ham it up and start the assembly with a bit of fun. She didn't disappoint me. She never did. She stuck her right thumb in her mouth, and twirled her hair with her other hand as if to imitate a small toddler. This brought on a fit of laughter from the audience.

After the finale of the happy birthday song, I asked everyone if they had seen the recent TV ads sponsored by the American Cancer Society in which cancer survivors share how grateful they are to be able to celebrate one more birthday. A few students and adults raised their hands.

"You don't have to be a cancer patient or survivor to appreciate one more birthday or to appreciate each day of life. We can all do that, but we must be aware and lead grateful lives," I shared. " That's why we are here today. To celebrate life, to mark the end of not only my cancer journey but also the journey you have been on with me. So let the celebrating begin!" The room exploded with cheers and applause.

"I'd like to call up Nick, a former student of mine," I continued.
Nick was sitting in the back of the room with the older students. He had a puzzled look on his face as he walked to the front of the room and took a stance by my side.

"In five days Nick and I have something special to celebrate," I said. "Nick, tell everyone what that will be."

Nick peered at me with a look that said, "Now I get it."

"It's our birthday," he explained.

In almost thirty years of teaching, Nick was the only student I had ever known who shared the same birth date as me.

"Yep, that's right. Nick and I are twins because we have the same birthday," I said as Nick gave me a mischievous grin and nodded his head in agreement. The audience quickly caught on to our antics and laughter filled the room again.

As if right on cue, a kindergartener in the front row blurted out, "You're not twins!"

"Why not? We have the same birthday," I responded.

"Because you're too old, Mrs. Pottorff," the kindergartener explained as laughter echoed throughout the room.

"You are absolutely right," I assured the young student. "Even though Nick and I have the same birth date, we were not born in the same year, and we are not the same age. Let's just say that I am a teeny bit older than Nick."

I thanked Nick for his help and gave him a quick hug before he returned to his spot in the back of the room.

"Like Nick and me, all of us have things in common and things which make us different. That is how it is with cancer patients. We have things in common and things, which are different. You all know about my cancer journey, and today I have invited Mrs. Hodges (our previous art teacher and a breast cancer survivor) to share about her battle with cancer."

Applause broke out to honor the beloved teacher as she walked to the front of the room. You could hear a pin drop as she shared her cancer journey from diagnosis to her current treatment. She drew on everyone's emotions as she explained the side effects of chemotherapy including losing her hair. She expertly brought her story full circle by pointing out how well she felt and that her gorgeous hair had grown back. She ended by sharing her thoughts regarding finding a cure for cancer by working together. Before she returned to her seat, I came to the front of the room to give the precious art teacher a heartfelt hug.

"Even though we were both diagnosed with breast cancer, Mrs. Hodges' and my journeys were different. Because my cancer was caught at an earlier stage, I didn't go through chemotherapy. I didn't lose my hair, and I don't take the same medications as Mrs. Hodges. As you can see, our journeys were very different. People who love and care about cancer patients and cancer survivors also have very different experiences and journeys as well. How many of you know someone who has been diagnosed cancer?" I asked.

Everyone in the room, students and adults, raised their hands.

"Everyone's hand should be up because you all know Mrs. Hodges, and you all know me," I continued. "I know many of you know other people who have fought cancer. Maybe it is a grandparent, an aunt or uncle, a neighbor or family friend. Cancer comes into all of our lives. I would like to thank some people who have traveled with me on my cancer journey. First, I would like to thank all the students in my class. Please stand and be recognized."

Once again the room exploded with cheers and applause as the students in our class stood. I could see their sense of pride in their facial expressions and their body language. They had every right to be proud. For such young people, they had been through so much in the last few months. They had taken part in discussions about mortality, the physical aspects of cancer, our purposes in life, empathy, and social awareness. Through it all, they had the nagging question in the back of their minds, "Is my teacher going to be okay?" On this journey, they had given me an unlimited amount of unconditional love and understanding. On days when I felt too exhausted to walk or even sit in a chair for an extended period of time, their hugs, laughter, and encouraging words gave me strength and carried me through the rough spots. I could never thank them enough. Having them stand and be recognized at an assembly was the least I could do.

Up until this point in the assembly, I had been able to keep my emotions under control. However, seeing my students standing there and knowing how much they had done for me, opened the floodgates, and the tears began to flow. I had anticipated this would happen and had tucked several tissues in my

I knew it. My hypothesis was correct. "I had a brother who died of cancer, too," I told her. "I admire you for what you do to help other people."

"I really miss my brother," she added as tears welled up in her eyes. "We were close and had a good relationship. I feel this is a good way to keep his memory alive."

That afternoon we shared about our brothers, about missing them, and about dealing with cancer. From that day on, Lavonne and I had a bond almost like a sisterhood.

I would often put on a pair of plastic gloves and help her serve a meal when the line was long during our lunch period. She would ask me to do "mini commercials" for foods that were new on the menu. It was often a new kind of pizza or cookie that was being offered. We would do a clapping sequence to get the students' attention, then I would start the commercial by devouring the new food and exclaiming how delicious it was. I had no problem eating free pizza and cookies. It wasn't like Lavonne was asking me to eat prunes or liver. Over the years, we had a lot of fun with our mini food commercials, but our bond wasn't over food. It was the fact that cancer had taken our brothers and left us feeling helpless and empty, but we had found strength in that commonality. We had also found hope and friendship.

I had spoken to Lavonne about sharing her story at the assembly. She was actually honored to be part of the project, stating it would be one more way to honor her brother. Knowing she would be working in the kitchen during the assembly, we had

143

worked out a plan that she would keep the kitchen door open, and she would come out to share her story when she heard me call her name.

Our plan worked perfectly. On cue, she emerged from the kitchen and walked to the area near the stage. Lavonne passionately shared her brother's story and that of her donating her hair to Locks of Love. When she finished, there wasn't a dry eye in the room.

Lavonne had kept her story a secret for so long. I wanted that to be over not only for her, but for so many other people sitting in that room. The time to talk about cancer was now. I no longer wanted to refer to it as "the 'C' word." I no longer wanted to keep silent about cancer because it scared people or made them feel uncomfortable. All that silence just gave cancer more power over all of us. As far as I was concerned, those days were over. As of today, we were taking the power back.

"If there is anyone else in this room who has donated their hair to Locks of Love, please come forward and join Ms. Lavonne to be recognized," I instructed.

I had suspected about six kids in the student population had donated their hair, but, to my surprise, fifteen students came forward to proudly stand by Lavonne to be recognized. This time it was Lavonne who let the tears flow freely.

As Lavonne returned to the kitchen and the brave students returned to their spots in the audience, I took the opportunity to remind everyone that we had been on a journey together.

"I think Ms. Lavonne and the fifteen young people who were just up here are perfect examples that none of us have to be victims of cancer. Through our actions, we can be victors. We can win the battle against cancer. How? By helping others. Ms. Lavonne and those students gave up their hair so that cancer patients could have wigs to wear," I shared. "But let's not forget that we as a school community raised $150 to purchase skin care products for cancer patients who are going through radiation treatments. We donated $643 to The House That Love Built so that cancer patients and their families have a place to live while going through treatments." The room exploded with cheers and applause.

"I want all of you to remember that we can fight cancer through our actions, by helping others, and by working together. But there is one more thing we can do. Omri the Pig is going to tell you what that 'one more thing" is on this short video," I told them.

Through God's intervention, I had "accidentally" found a video on YouTube, which playfully showcased my last point. In the video, Omri the Pig desperately wants the cookies in a jar on top of a refrigerator. He attempts several comical methods to obtain the alluring cookies, but unfortunately, he continues to fail. Finally, the cookie jar falls to the floor, but Omri soon discovers he has one more obstacle to overcome before he can enjoy the delicious treats. When the video ended and the laughter subsided, I shared a few final thoughts.

"The last component of our battle against cancer is persistence. Just like Omri the Pig, we must never give up on our quest to find the cause and the cure for cancer. Do we all agree?"

Once again the room echoed with cheers and applause.

"We will end our assembly out at the bell tower. I invite you to join me there," I instructed.

Once everyone had gathered at the tower, I took the opportunity to explain the significance of ringing the bell.

"This afternoon will be my last radiation treatment. After that treatment, I will ring a bell in the hall of the cancer center to signify the end of my cancer journey and the beginning of a new journey as a cancer free person. I know I didn't go on this journey alone. All of you traveled with me. I wanted to ring our school bell to signify the end of your journeys and the beginning of new ones for you. Hopefully on the journey with me, you have learned something. Maybe you learned that it is okay to talk about cancer. Maybe you learned a lesson about how it feels to help other people. Perhaps you learned how much we can accomplish together rather than alone. Whatever you learned, I hope it made you a better person, and it will help you on the new journey you will start today. Mrs. Hodges, please ring the bell."

Ginger Hodges was standing poised and ready on the side of the bell tower. On command, she rang it three times with all the passion and gusto she could muster. I raised my arms to form a gigantic "V" and an ear splitting victory cheer followed.

This is for You, God. I thought to myself. *This is for You.* Even though I was afraid, I had done what God had asked me. He had given me a plan. He was there with me every step of the way. All I had to do was open my mouth, and He supplied the words.

It wasn't until several days later I realized the breadth and depth of God's plan. I had assumed the messages in the assembly were intended for the school community, but I soon found out the messages were far reaching. A few friends of mine who taught at different schools within the district had emailed me, sharing they had watched the video of the assembly on the district's website. I was shocked. I hadn't realized there was a video. News of the video spread, and, by the end of the week, a Denver Post reporter called to interview me. God had a plan for the message to reach more people than I had ever anticipated, but He needed someone to initiate that plan. That someone was me, but God gave me a choice in the situation.

The assembly and the events that followed reminded me of what I call the "ripple effect." When I was a young girl, my brother and I loved to throw rocks into the lake, which bordered our farm. We loved to hear the plop as each rock entered the water, and we loved to watch the splash. It wasn't until I was older that I recognized the beauty of the ripples each stone created as the energy from the falling stone was transferred to the water. It created small waves or ripples, which reached all the way to the shore. It was my hope and hopefully part of God's plan that the energy from my cancer journey and from the assembly reached many people who needed to hear the message. Just like the ripples, which start from the rock, sometimes we don't realize how far our influence and energy can reach, perhaps, at times, all the way to the shore.

The Bell Tower Ceremony

Chapter 15
One Chapter Ends; Another Begins

My entire family had been on this journey, so I had invited them to join me to celebrate my last radiation treatment. I picked Landon up from his classroom and signed him out at the office before we left school that afternoon. Greg was picking up Sierra at her school, and we were all meeting at the cancer center at 3 p.m.

Greg and the kids sat in the waiting room as I went into the treatment room. Once in the room I shared with the peeps that I hadn't brought them a sweet treat today but a gift for each one of them. I had purchased a unique necklace for each lady; a piece of jewelry I felt symbolized each woman's individual personality. I also included a handwritten thank you note expressing my eternal gratitude.

"I want you to open these gifts after I leave today," I explained. "If you open them now, trust me, we are all going to cry."

"I think we're going to cry anyway," Dana confessed.

"I wish there was a way we could keep you around," Rose added.

"You could zap my left breast with radiation for twenty-eight days," I responded. We all laughed.

As usual, the treatment was over in a matter of minutes, but this time instead of me leaving the room alone, the peeps followed me into the hall.

Jennifer was working in the other treatment room that day. She came out to tell me good-bye.

"What are we going to do without you?" she whispered as she gave me a big hug.

"Probably lose weight," I told her, referring to all the sugary treats I had brought them over the last several weeks.

My family joined us by the bell, and I introduced everyone. As the small group of cheerleaders looked on, I grabbed the leather strap of the bell with a death grip then pulled with all the energy I could muster. *Take that, cancer! This is for Dad, for Steve, and for Barb!*

I whacked the bell again. This is for everything you (cancer) have put the people I love through-my family, my friends, my students.

The final blow to the bell was for me. The sound echoed through the hall as if it were a declaration of my freedom and independence. I was cancer free, free from surgeries, free from treatments, and free from fear. I had been in the boxing ring with cancer, my gloves up, and ready for battle. I'd suffered the initial punch to the head and few to the gut, but I had learned from my mistakes. I had kept on fighting. Today the knock out bell had sounded, and I was the one left standing.

We took a few photos to commemorate the event. I hugged the peeps good-bye then my family and I left to enjoy a celebratory meal. Whenever I returned to the cancer center for my annual exams, I would always stop to say hello to the peeps, bringing them sweet treats and heartfelt hugs. One

150

by one the peeps left to take other jobs until there was no one left in the radiation department that I knew.

When we returned home on the evening of my last radiation treatment, I removed my treatment calendar from the refrigerator door. Taking a pen I marked an "x", the last "x", on the calendar. Barb's words, "You can do this," repeated in my mind. I took the calendar into the master bedroom and placed it in the gray pocket folder I had been given during my radiation orientation. As I closed the folder, I thought how symbolic that action was. I thought I was actually closing the cancer part of my life, but little did I know it wasn't the end of the book just the end of a chapter. There were still more chapters waiting to unfold.

In fact, the next chapter revealed itself to us the following week. I was in the kitchen preparing the evening meal when Greg arrived home from work with a wonderful expression on his face.

"I've got something to tell you," he began. "You are not going to believe this. We have a cancer insurance policy. I bought it several years ago. I thought it would be a good idea since there is a history of cancer in both of our families. The premium is small, and it comes out of my paycheck automatically each month so I don't think much about it. Every January the insurance agent stops by school to review all of our policies with me. Usually he wants to know if I need to make any changes, or if I want t keep things as is. He showed up today after school and was summarizing everything, and that's when I realized we have a cancer insurance policy!"

I was shocked. I had to let his words soak in before I could speak.

"I had no idea. You never told me," I finally stammered.

"It didn't seem like a big deal so I never mentioned it before," Greg explained.

"What does this mean? What do we do now?" I questioned.

"We go to the company's website and print out the forms we need to complete then we send those in along with receipts, bills, and cancelled checks. If we do all of that then we should be reimbursed for any expenses for your cancer treatments that were not covered by our regular health insurance."

I still couldn't believe what Greg was telling me. I shut off the burners on the stove and took a seat on one of the kitchen bar stools.

"Isn't this great news?" Greg continued.

"It is great news," I added. "But I still can't believe it. With such a history of cancer in both of our families, I can't believe any insurance company would offer us cancer insurance. I'm glad we will be able to replenish our emergency fund, but I also assume once we put in the claim, the company will drop us."

"No, the agent assured me we wouldn't be dropped. His words were, 'Of course, we are in business to make a profit, but we are also in business to help people when they need it the most,'" Greg explained.

I had received the exact opposite response from our health insurance company. To them I was just a number, a number with a large price tag. I was constantly receiving letters from the company stating all the procedures and medications that were not covered in our policy along with "friendly" reminders of our gigantic deductible.

Then out of nowhere pops up an American Family Insurance agent telling us all the things their company would do to help us. To me, it was a miracle and one more component of God's plan.

After the evening meal that night, Greg and I sat at the computer to print out the required insurance forms, actually it was more like a booklet so we organized it into a three-ringed binder. I could tell the process was going to be a huge undertaking, but it seemed doable if we took it one step at a time. It actually took over four months to complete the forms, obtain letters from all the doctors who were involved with my case, and to organize the bill statements, receipts, and cancelled checks. My persistence and hard work literally paid off. By June, we cashed a check from the insurance company, and our emergency fund was replenished.

Although my physical treatments for cancer were over, my internal healing was just beginning. It was true that a chapter in my life was coming to an end, but the next chapter was just beginning

Chapter 16
Humanness

With my radiation treatments completed, the school year coming to an end, and our emergency fund replenished, the next logical step in the sequence of events seemed to be to go on our victory trip to any where in the world.

Greg had given the trip to me for Christmas, and it was now June so I had been thinking about the trip and our destination for several months. I finally decided I wanted to go to France to see the art at the Louvre in Paris. I believed I could gain some insight into the age-old question of "What is the meaning of life?" by experiencing what people from all over the world viewed as beautiful masterpieces. If I could see what others treasured and valued, perhaps that would help me decide what I treasured and valued.

Mid June, we shipped the kids off to Grandma's house with the hope that Landon would fulfill his dream of drinking coffee and eating desserts on a daily basis, and Sierra could enjoy the thrill of driving Grandma's car.

Greg and I had hopes, too. We hoped this trip would offer us time to relax after the stress filled months we had endured. We were looking forward to spending time together, which was something we hadn't done in several years. I was on a personal quest searching for meaning in my life. I wanted to reach beyond the boundaries, which created my life, to see what was important to people around the world.

Although this wasn't our first trip to another country, Greg and I were excited and filled with anticipation as we stepped off the plane and entered the airport in Paris. We quickly found the transportation we needed to take us to our hotel. Once there, we unpacked then slept for most of the afternoon. When we woke, it was about time for the evening meal, so we headed to the hotel lobby to search for a place to eat. We struck up a conversation with a couple. They told us they had spent the day site seeing just by taking the local bus. We thought we could take the bus to find a nice place to enjoy the evening meal. We carefully followed the directions they had given us but never did find a bus stop. We continued walking until we were totally and utterly lost.

Finally, out of complete desperation, we stopped a young man and asked for directions to the Arc de Triomphe, which is a famous architectural and historical landmark. God was truly looking out for us when we realized the first person we asked for help spoke English. We followed his detailed directions and within thirty minutes found ourselves at our desired destination.

As the name implies, the Arc de Triomphe is a majestic stone symbol of France's victories in many conflicts including the French Revolution, the Napoleonic Wars, World War I, and World War II. Throughout history many victory parades triumphantly traveled through and around the famous arc. Ironically, we were now parading through the arc's columns triumphantly celebrating our victory over cancer but also the ominous streets of Paris. Fortunately, we had realized that battles are often won only with the help of allies. The cancer battle was won through a team effort, and today our ally had been the kind young man who offered us directions to our current location.

With photos of our conquest conveniently stored in our digital camera, we realized a victory celebration is not complete without consuming large quantities of food and drink. A quaint restaurant across the street seemed to be the answer to this conundrum. Our laughter intertwined with the rumble of car motors, as we ventured across the busy throughway to the entrance of an inviting French bistro.

Once we were seated, a petite man in his late fifties arrived at our table to offer us menus. We quickly discovered he didn't speak English, and we, of course, didn't speak French. Although we didn't share a common language, we soon realized we shared something that was even more important . . .we were human beings. Through gestures, facial expressions, and simply by pointing at the menu, we were able to order entrees and beverages. Even though our dining choices had been made, we had no idea what we were going to eat until it arrived at our table. When our mystery meal arrived, it was hot and satisfied our hunger. The food was actually mediocre at best, but what made the meal so enjoyable was our waiter.

The waiter periodically returned to our table to check on us and refill our water glasses. Each time we would communicate with thumbs up, okay signs, smiles, and copious amounts of laughter. In fact, I hadn't laughed that much in a very long time. Who would have thought that people, who didn't even share the same language, could have so much fun?

Near the end of our dining experience, our fun-loving waiter suggested a dessert by pointing at the menu and giving us an enthusiastic two thumbs up and a clever wink. The recommended dessert was exquisite. After paying the bill and bidding our friendly server good-bye, we ventured out to the street. We had learned our lesson about trying to independently navigate our way through the streets of Paris, so we successfully hailed a cab. Although our driver didn't speak English, we simply told him the name of our hotel, and that was all the information he needed.

During the cab ride, I replayed the afternoon's events in my head. A smile spread across my face as I remembered the young man who seemed genuinely happy to help us with directions. I actually chuckled while reminiscing about our interactions with our waiter. Now I was traveling back to our hotel with a cab driver who didn't speak English. I finally decided we didn't need to speak the same language in order to communicate. All we needed was our "humanness."

Chapter 17
Fellow Travelers

Excited to begin our adventure, Greg and I were the first people to board the tour bus the next morning. Soon our fellow travelers began to board the bus and introduce themselves.

Our first encounter was with a lovely couple in their early fifties from England. In their beautiful British accents, they explained to us that they were both doctors and traveling was their hobby. They took a minimum of two international trips each year. We were astounded when they listed all the countries they had visited.

Our next interaction was with a family from the United States, which consisted of a grandfather, a grandmother, and four elementary aged grandchildren. The grandparents explained to us that they wanted to give their grandkids something they never had as children, which was the opportunity to see the world and experience different people and cultures. Each summer they took their brood of grandchildren to a new destination. This yearly adventure gave them the opportunity to bond over shared experiences. It also gave the parents of the children the opportunity to continue working without the worry of summer childcare. Just like the British couple, the members of this family were well-seasoned, veteran, world travelers.

Our conversation with the family was briefly interrupted by the sound of laughter at the entrance of the bus. The cackling was coming from a group of four older ladies. When they weren't laughing, they were speaking with the most delightful southern accents. As they made their way down the center aisle to the back of the bus, they stopped to introduce themselves to the people who were already seated. Through these conversations, we learned the ladies were either widows or had husbands who didn't appreciate the joys of traveling. These circumstances lead the ladies to develop their "annual girls' trip." The energy this group exuded was incredible.

Our next traveling companions to enter the bus were two beautiful, shy young women in their twenties. Dressed in jean shorts, t-shirts, and flip-flops, they appeared to be ready for a summer adventure. Later we would learn they were childhood friends from South Korea.

A few more passengers filtered into the bus, quickly claiming their seats without speaking to anyone.

"We are waiting on two members of our group before we can begin our tour," Simeon our tour guide informed us over the intercom.

Immediately after he had made this announcement, a middle-aged man and woman emerged from the hotel and nonchalantly walked across the parking lot toward our tour bus. Upon entering the bus, they checked in with our tour guide who efficiently checked their names off the roster attached to a clipboard. They quickly took the only available seat, the front seat by the door.

Simeon the tour guide grabbed the microphone once again. "This is the perfect time to discuss what happens when someone is late," he began. "Not only are you late, but you make everyone else late as well. We are always on a tight schedule to travel to our various venues, and often we must join other tours once we arrive at our destinations. For these reasons and as a common courtesy for your fellow travelers, I ask that you adhere to the times on our daily schedules."

How embarrassing for the couple who was late. I glanced in their direction only to see them talking to each other as the tour guide was speaking. Obviously his " don't be late" speech was having no effect on them.

"Did I mention the consequence for being late?" Simeon continued. "If you are late you will be required to sing a song chosen by your fellow travelers. Today there will be no singing because I hadn't explained the rules regarding tardiness yet." He glanced at the couple in the front seat who had stopped talking long enough to flash him two fake smiles. My intuition told me these two were going to be singing a lot on this trip. At least I hoped they had good voices.

Fellow Travelers

Chapter 18
Stop the Bus!

As I surveyed the bus on the morning of our first thering, I felt like I was on a field trip only this time I was a student instead of one of the supervising teachers. The tour guide's rendition of bus rules added to the field trip vibe. How many times had I explained not to get out of your seat while the bus was moving, no appendages should be hanging out the windows, and of course, don't throw trash on the floor?

Our tour guide Simeon was a petite person probably in his thirties with dark hair and brown eyes. For a person who had a small physical stature, he had a gigantic personality. He spoke with his entire body, bouncing up and down and using his hands to illustrate his words. His love for his country simply oozed from every part of his being.

After briefly speaking about himself, he eloquently introduced our guest guide for the day. An elegant white-haired woman suddenly appeared at the front of the bus. She skillfully took the microphone from our regular tour guide and began speaking.

The only thing that was average about her was her height. Her slender body made purposeful, graceful movements. Her voice was smooth, loud but breathy. Even the couple in the front seat who talked continually listened intently. She wore a tight fitting red knit top, white calf length slacks and a long silk white scarf wrapped around her neck. A pair of flat, strappy sandals completed her dignified, understated ensemble. Every thing about her indicated she was a timeless, classic beauty.

Her name was Nadine. She had spent her entire life, seventy-five years, in Paris. She wanted to share her love for the city with others, so she had been a tour guide for most of her adult life.

She shared with us that there would be times throughout the day when we would be able to explore on our own, and times when we would experience venues as a group. Her one request was when she raised her hand, we would all gather around her and give her our full attention. *Sounds reasonable to me. Let the adventure begin.* I, like Nadine, wanted to fall in love with the city of Paris.

"Our first stop will be the Eiffel Tower," Nadine informed us.

I wanted to jump out of my seat, fling my arms into the air, and shout, "Hurray!" A quick glance around the bus revealed that no one else was exhibiting public displays of excitement, so I decided to contain my emotion to the privacy of my own imagination.

The bus doors snapped shut, and in a matter of minutes, we were traversing along the streets of Paris. When the Eiffel Tower first appeared on the horizon, my heartbeat quickened. By the time the bus stopped in a parking lot with the tower looming in the distance, my heart was racing. I, too, wanted to race. I wanted to race out of the bus to one of the world's most famous landmarks to explore and wonder at all of its beautiful idiosyncrasies. Instead, I was trapped inside a metal enclosure with its doors clenched shut like fingers forming a fist around my curiosity.

Our Parisian guide took this opportunity to share a few facts about the tower waiting just beyond our reach. While her knowledge was extensive and astonishing, I just wanted to exit the bus and experience the Eiffel Tower for myself.

"Our schedule doesn't permit us to go to the top of the Eiffel Tower today," Nadine told us. "We will stop here momentarily for you to stretch your legs and take a few photographs. Please look at your watches and return to the bus in twenty minutes."

Wait. What? We're not going to the top of the Eiffel Tower? That's crazy! In a panic, I glanced around the bus to see if anyone else was as shocked about this development as I was. They seemed unaffected by the announcement. Sitting across the aisle was the couple with the grandkids. They must have seen the look of disbelief on my face.

"It's not all its cracked up to be," the granddad tried to assure me.

"He's right," his wife continued. " We were here a few years ago without the grandkids. It was just the two of us. We waited in line for hours to get on the elevator, spent some time on the top enjoying the views, then waited in line for hours to ride the elevator down. It was an all day affair."

"They're right." The lady from the British couple chimed in. "It's not as spectacular as you think it is."

Sure, that is easy for them to say. They had been to top. I had traveled halfway around the world, and now I wasn't going to have that opportunity. I mentally kicked myself. At least I was here! I decided to go out and make the best use of those twenty minutes the guide had given us.

Greg and I exited the bus and began snapping a plethora of photos of the world famous landmark. Mission accomplished. It wasn't the mission I had originally intended to go on, but it was a mission nonetheless.

Once back on the bus, we continued our journey motoring through the streets of Paris. We drove around the Arc de Triomphe but didn't stop. I was okay with that since we had explored it the night before.

We drove by the Pot des Art Bridge, also known as the Love Lock Bridge. Visitors attach padlocks to the railings and wire fencing on the sides of the bridge. Part of this ritual is to then throw the keys to the locks into the Seine River as a profession of love for another human being. How romantic, I mused. It would have been a memorable experience if we could have stopped to add our own padlocks to the collection or, at least, to have been able to touch and admire a few of the locks. But it wasn't meant to be. We sped by with only a fleeting glance at the bridge, which symbolized love in "the city of love."

We also sped by the Louvre with its beautiful, glass pyramid majestically standing in the courtyard inviting us to stop and admire the world's largest collection of artwork. Actually, I was at peace with not stopping because I knew we were going to tour the museum on our last day.

We sped by the Les Invalides, whichis a complex
of buildings ordered by King Louis XIV to be
constructed as a home and hospital for war veterans.
Eventually, it also became a museum for military
and historical artifacts. The domed structure at the
center of the complex reminded me of the state
capital building in Denver. It housed the remains of
Napoleon Bonaparte and many of his possessions.
How exciting it would have been to stop and walk
on the same ground that Napoleon was buried in or
to view items he had touched and used. Instead, we
whizzed by in a hurry to reach our next scheduled
destination.

I began to realize this was how bus tours worked.
I didn't know since I had never been on one before.
I guessed you drove by famous places and looked at
them from your window. Unfortunately, I wanted
to explore and experience these places, not just look
at them. This bus tour seemed to be a metaphor for
life. Everything just passes by in one giant blur,
and the whole time you are wondering when is
everything going to stop for a bit so I can enjoy the
precious moments?

Stop the bus! I wanted to scream as we raced by
the La Sorbonne. This was also a complex of
majestic buildings with stunning architectural
elements. From 1253 until the present, it has
housed the world's oldest university. How
wonderful it would have been for two teachers from
Colorado to stand on the steps of the world's first
university, but that wasn't in the plans for the day.

I was wallowing in self-pity when something
miraculously happened . . . the bus stopped! Then I

saw the reason for our abrupt halt. The view from the front windshield took my breath away. There before me in all of its stately, magnificent beauty was the Notre Dame Cathedral.

We were parked in front of the most famous cathedral in the world! Would this be the place where I would experience goose bumps? Would this be the place where I would discover meaning in my life? I intended to get off the bus and find out. But wait. I couldn't just go and spontaneously find the meaning of life. This was a bus tour for heavens sake. There was a price to pay for such knowledge. There were rules, regulations, and protocols attached to all of this.

Once we disembarked, I surveyed the surroundings. There were hundreds of people not rambling about but in neatly formed single file lines, which stretched into the street in all directions. A hum-like murmur permeated the air. It was the sound of people talking in several different languages yet creating one single sound. How magical.

I desperately searched the environment to find something familiar. At last I found it. There was our silver-haired tour guide with her arm outstretched to the sky and in her hand was the white silk scarf previously tied around her neck. It waved in the wind like the flame of a torch beckoning us to join her for a group learning experience. We obediently huddled around our guide as she prepared to explain the history and unique features of the famous cathedral.

It was time to pay the price for the possibility of learning the meaning of life. We all had to listen to an informative speech, which had to be given outside because once inside we would not be able to speak. Silence would be our way to show reverence and respect.

The work on the Notre Dame Cathedral continued from 1163 until 1345. The flying buttresses and center spire were unique exterior features. The other features included stained glass windows, marble floors, stone sculptures, intricate altars, and the magnificent organ.

At the end of her speech Nadine turned toward the church and walked directly to the front entrance bypassing the numerous lines of people patiently waiting for their turns to enter.

Can we do this? Just go in front of all these people? Someone else must have been thinking the same thing and actually verbalized it to our guide.

"That's the beauty of being on a tour," Nadine responded. "I've been here thousands of times. The people who work here all know me. Now, come along." Then she confidently and defiantly led us through the front door.

A few moments passed before my eyes adjusted to the darkness. The musty, cold air engulfed my body. The silence was broken by the sound of people's shoes clicking against the stone floors. I admired the windows, the altars, the statues, the architecture, and the artwork. I tried to find inspiration in the religious concepts this cathedral symbolized. I waited for the anticipated goose bumps but none formed. I waited for that fairy tale "ah ha moment" when the meaning of life would be revealed to me, but it alluded me once again.

We spent about n hour exploring the cathedral independently. When we finally emerged from the holy structure, the sunlight seemed to blind us. In silence we boarded the bus, which had become our home away from home. The silence seemed to be an
expression of my disappointment, but why was everyone else so quiet? Were they disappointed as well? I would never know the answer to that question.

As we travel to our next designated destination for lunch, I decided to replace my increasing collection of little negative thoughts with one, big, positive thought . . . at least the bus had stopped!

Chapter 19
Let Them Eat Cake

Cake was not part of our lunch experience. In fact, there wasn't even anything close to cake. Lunch consisted of vegetable soup, crusty French bread, and a glass of room temperature water. Fortunately, dunking the bread into the soup allowed the liquid to permeate the fibers of the bread to soften it. Unfortunately, there was no such remedy for the water. It was hopeless. Greg and I don't drink coffee, tea, or soda. We are water people, plain and simple. All we ask is that the water has ice in it. From what we had experienced so far, we assumed that ice didn't exist in France.

After lunch, we boarded the bus to begin our twelve mile journey out to the French countryside in order to tour the Palace at Versailles. This massive, opulent place was the main residence of the French royalty from 1682, under King Louis XIV, until the start of the French Revolution in 1789, under King Louis XVI.

When we reached our destination, an eighty-seven yard golden gate covered with over one hundred thousand gold leaves greeted us. The intricate metal work with its regal crowns, delicate leaves, pointed spires, arrows, golden vines, and flowers was a mixture of beautiful artwork and stately functionality. As we drove through the open gate, we were transported from the harsh world of reality lived by commoners, to the lavish, luxurious world lived by the nobility of the past. Enormous tour buses filled the gigantic parking lot, which stretched before us. Passengers were loading and unloading like ants scurrying to and from various ant holes. Approximately ten million people visit the Palace at Versailles a year, and I was totally convinced all of those people were in the parking lot on that day.

While waiting to depart from our bus, I looked out the window at the monumental structure before us. It appeared to be a series of connected, multi-storied rectangular buildings. Later we would learn the exterior included 2,143 windows and 1,252 chimneys. The interior consisted of over seven hundred rooms and sixty-seven staircases. But it wasn't the size or the architectural features I was thinking about. I was thinking about what fascinating tales of romance, betrayal, intrigue, and espionage must have occurred here. If only these walls could talk.

The only talking we heard was from our lovely silver-haired Nadine. She gathered us together outside the bus to share a few facts about the palace. This lavish palace actually had humble beginnings. King Louis XIII found the forests in the region to be excellent hunting grounds. His admiration for the area grew until he eventually built a hunting lodge in 1624. In 1632 he purchased additional land in order to expand the lodge into a chateau with surrounding gardens. King Louis XIV had enjoyed Versailles as a boy. During his time as the King of France, he expanded the chateau until it became one of the world's largest palaces. In 1683 the royal court and government was officially moved from Paris to Versailles. King Louis XIV believed this move would help him maintain his power by ensuring that all his advisors and provincial rulers would be kept close to him. In other words, he didn't trust any one. His son King Louis XV continued expanding the palace, as did his son King Louis XVI until the beginning of the French Revolution.

With our brief history of the palace complete, Nadine explained that once we were inside, she would be leading our tour. In case we became separated, she told us what time to meet back at the bus for our departure. Then she quickly and confidently led us to the front of a ginormous line to begin our tour.

The interior of the Palace at Versailles must be experienced in person in order to truly appreciate its grandeur. Photographs simply cannot do it justice. Not only were the sizes of the rooms impressive, but every nuance as well. The walls were covered with elaborately designed wallpaper. Enormous paintings in gilded frames showcased the elements of culture for time periods of the past. The humans portrayed in the fresco paintings on the ceilings seemed to be able to cross the boundaries of reality and fantasy. The color, weight, and texture of the tapestries, which covered the windows and furniture, created an air of elegance, refinement, and sophistication. From the marble floors to the crystal chandeliers, each detail of the palace depicted the essence of wealth, and prosperity, which is exactly what the French nobility of the past wanted their guests and visitors to experience and believe. Perhaps wealth and prosperity flourished inside the palace walls, but beyond the palace's golden gates, hunger, poverty, and despair were the norm.

This inequitable way of living continued until the French Revolution. During this uprising of the lower class, the Palace at Versailles became a symbol of the skewed economy and government. The once impenetrable golden gate was broken. During the years that followed much of the furniture, artwork, and furnishings were sold, and the palace fell into a state of disrepair.

This was followed by a period in which there were several attempts to restore the historic site. In 1833, sections of the palace became a museum. From 1925 until 1928, the American Rockefeller Foundation donated thirty million dollars to repair and restore Versailles. From 1952 until 1980, the French government tried to acquire as much of the original furniture, furnishings, and artwork that had been dispersed at the time of the French Revolution as possible.

Currently, the Palace of Versailles is owned by the French state. It has been run as a public establishment with an independent administration and management supervised by the French Ministry of Culture.

With the tour of the palace complete, we were instructed to independently explore the vast surrounding gardens. These gardens are famous for the manicured, maze-like lawns, the variety of trees and flowers, exquisite statues and sculptures, and mesmerizing fountains. As the palace and gardens continued to expand throughout the years, so did the need for water. In the early years, water was pumped from nearby ponds using gravitational hydraulics. As time progressed so did the methods of solving the need for additional water. These methods included reservoirs, water towers, pumps, waterwheels, and windmills. Obviously it wasn't a piece of cake supplying Versailles' unquenchable thirst for water. In my mind it all boiled down to the classic question of why does man feel the need to manipulate nature? Why can't human beings simply enjoy the beauty of nature the way it is?

Another question quickly came to mind as we ventured across the gardens to the public restrooms. Why would a structure with 721,182 square feet only have two public restrooms, one for women and one for men? That was insane, and so were the lines to use these coveted facilities.

I began the day searching for answers, but I had found only more questions. On the bus ride back to our hotel, I pondered these questions. I had hoped that by visiting Notre Dame, one of the most famous religious structures in the world, I would receive a message from God about finding meaning in my life. Instead what I saw was a cathedral that took two hundred eighty-two years to complete. While religious and government leaders were funneling money into this structure, people were struggling to pay for the basic necessities of life including food, shelter, and clothing. Money spent on stained glass windows, marble sculptures and floors, and elaborate altars, could have been used to improve the lives of the destitute and poor. Did people of the past truly believe God valued things more than people? I think the answer to this question is what is often referred to as "a no brainer." Of course, God values people more than things. If we know this fact to be true then why were human beings of that era building things instead of caring for people? Why are we still doing that today?

How could the royalty of France, the leaders of the country, live such self indulgent, opulent, lavish lives while the common people lived in poverty, dying of starvation, exposure, and diseases?

Perhaps the answer could be found in a quote, which is often mistakenly attributed to Marie Antoinette. No matter who said the words, the meaning is still clear. There is a disconnect between the rich and the poor. The affluent are either oblivious or insensitive to the needs and realities of the less fortunate. As the story or legend goes, when a member of the French royalty was asked what the common people should eat when they had no bread, the response was let them eat cake.

The Palace at Versailles

Chapter 20
Mother Nature: Friend or Foe

Have you ever noticed that even though people don't have assigned seats in church, they always seem to sit in the same place? That's how it was on the tour bus. Greg and I were the first ones on the bus the next morning, and we sat in the same seat as the previous day, smack dab in the middle of the bus.

The next travelers to enter the bus were the British couple, but instead of going to their "assigned seat" they stopped in the aisle in front of us.

"You are from Colorado Springs, right?" the lady asked.

"Yes, we live near there," Greg responded.

"Is your home all right?" the gentlemen inquired.

"What do you mean?"

"There was a report on the news last night," the man continued. "There is a forest fire near Colorado Springs."

"We didn't watch the news last night or this morning," I shared.

"We didn't mean to alarm you," the woman said. "We were just concerned about your home."

"Thank you for bringing this to our attention," Greg told her. "We'll try to call some of our friends to check on the status of the fire."

As the couple moved down the aisle and sat a few seats behind us, Greg and I continued our conversation.

"At least the kids are safe at your mom's house," I began. We lived on the east side of the Colorado mountains, and Greg's mom lived on the west side, which is often referred to as the Western Slope.

"I would think our friends or some of our neighbors would have called us if our neighborhood was in danger," Greg added.

Together we decided we would call a few friends later in the evening, so it would be mid-morning where they lived. Most of our friends were teachers so they were on summer break. Worrying seemed to be just a waste of time and energy, so we decided to enjoy the rest of the day.

Apparently we were the only ones who hadn't watched the news because as each group entered the bus, they came directly to our seat and asked us about the status of our home. We were genuinely touched by their concern. Basically, we had only met everyone twenty-four hours ago.

We were anxious to begin our adventures for the day to take our minds off the fire near our home, but we were waiting for the same couple as yesterday. *Déjà vu!* Once again they emerged from the hotel entrance and meandered across the parking lot rolling their luggage behind them.

"You're ten minutes late. You will need to sing a song for your fellow travelers."
Simeon informed them as he glanced at this watch.

"What song would you like to hear this morning?" Simeon asked us.

"Three Blind Mice," someone blurted out.

The tardy pair stood by the driver and sang a few lines of the requested song before sitting in their "assigned seat" at the front of the bus.

Today we were headed to Giverny to tour the home and gardens of the impressionistic painter Claude Monet. Once we arrived at our scheduled destination, we would tour the area independently, so Simeon shared information about the famous painter and his home as we traveled down the highway.

In the spring of 1883, Monet and his large family rented the home and two acres of land surrounding it. He enjoyed the area so much that he purchased the home and land later that year. During the forty-three years Monet lived on the property, he adapted the house and garden areas to meet the needs of his family and his professional life.

Being the father of eight children, and the fact that Monet liked to entertain guests, led to the addition of two wings to the residence. Monet was very involved in the renovation of the home. He planned the large, colorful rooms, which completed the house. He was also very intentional about the exterior of the home. He wanted it to blend in with nature so he strategically planted vines, bushes, trees, and flowers to adorn the house.

His same hands-on approach was true for the gardens. He used his collection of botany books to help him design this outdoor area and purchase the plants. As Monet's wealth grew with the sale of his paintings, so did his gardens. He purchased more land, which bordered his property. Then he began a huge landscaping project, which included Japanese inspired bridges and lily ponds.

Monet was known for his paintings of the French countryside. He often painted the same landscape several times in an effort to capture the light at various times of the day or to capture a variety of colors with the changing seasons. He purposefully planned the gardens so he could continue painting landscapes without ever leaving his home. His intentional use of colors, textures, light, and reflections were evident in the environment around him, and the magic his paint created on his canvases.

The interesting talk Simeon had given made our travel time fly by, and before we knew it, we were at our destination. Once we exited the bus, we followed Simeon through a dark cement tunnel. When we emerged from the tunnel, it was as if we had been transported to another world.

We were surrounded by thick vegetation, which was reminiscent of a jungle. The vegetation covered every inch of the ground except the stone path we were walking on. The vibrant colors of the many flowers were contrasted with the green of the weeping willows, bushes, and deciduous trees. The walking path bordered a small stream. Just as Monet had planned, the surrounding plants and the turquoise sky were reflected in the mirror-like surface of the water, and the sunlight sparkled as if the water had been sprinkled with glitter. We stopped on an arched wooden bridge to soak in the beauty and to make a feeble attempt to capture it with our cameras.

Our self-guided tour of the home was interesting, but the gardens were absolutely captivating. We were drawn to them like a moth is drawn to a flame. We used our remaining time on the property to walk the paths through the gardens, enjoying the flowering plants, the famous lily ponds, the inviting bridges, and glistening river. I didn't have the "ah ha" moment I had been looking for, but I did feel calm, peaceful, and relaxed. What a wonderful life Claude Monet must have had here. No wonder he wanted to capture this tranquil beauty on his canvases.

I started to compare and contrast the gardens at Versailles with the gardens at Monet's home. Both were massive and beautiful. But the Versailles gardens seemed to be an example of man trying to control and manipulate nature. The many creative ways the French developed to quench the garden's insatiable thirst for water came to mind. The hedges and bushes that were trimmed to resemble objects and animals were other examples.

In contrast, the Monet gardens seemed to enhance nature. Even though the stream on the property was changed to create a series of lily ponds, the outcome created the illusion that nature, not man, had created these features. Even the buildings had been made to blend in with the natural surroundings through the use of vines, trees, brushes, and flowers. Monet had strategically selected all of the plants, and had purposely planned their placement, but it appeared this had all occurred naturally.

The garden had made me stop and ponder. How do we as humans learn to coexist with nature? Is nature something to be used, controlled, and exploited, or is it something to be valued, enhanced, and appreciated? These questions rumbled around in my mind as we traveled to our next stop, the Cathedral at Rouen.

Massive was the adjective that came to mind as our bus pulled into the parking lot of this famous church. The enormous structure towered over the entire town. The cathedral's spires appeared to pierce the sky. The monumental arches seemed to defy gravity. The large wooden doors gave the impression that giants could enter through them. This exquisite piece of architecture was absolutely breath taking.

The interior of this fascinating structure was just as phenomenal as the exterior. The use of light colored stone and the calculated placement of the windows illuminated every nook and cranny of this well-known church. Four story tall stone columns supported massive arches that crisscrossed the ceiling. The lengthy center aisle led to the splendid golden altar with an exquisite painting as the focal point.

We ventured throughout the interior in complete silence, exploring the alcoves and side chapels, and reading the plaques to gain an appreciation for the history of the church. At one time the structure was known as the tallest building in the world. Currently, it was known at the tallest church in France.

This place showcased my man versus nature theory. Humans had extracted the materials to build this church from nature, and nature had retaliated with a vengeance. Over the years, the building had been hit by lightning five times. It was damaged by fire several times and struck by two hurricanes. But the humans didn't give up or give in. For centuries the cathedral was in a constant state of expansion, rebuilding, or repair.

Soon our time at the cathedral came to an end. As we made our way toward the exit, we stopped to deposit a donation in a clear plastic box at the back of the church.

New cognitive challenges were forming in my mind. Why do humans spend so much time, energy, and money on building things rather than helping each other? Why is there a constant battle between humans and nature? When I used the word nature, was I really referring to God?

Our next stop was the picturesque port of Honfleur with the population of seven thousand residents. Honfleur is often referred to as the birthplace of impressionism. Artists like Courbet, Boudin, and Monet often came to Honfleur to sketch and paint. I could see why. From a distance, a beautiful handcrafted antique carousel welcomed us to the village. Boats with colorful hulls and sails were docked in the harbor, their reflections rippling in the mirror-like water. Flamboyant umbrellas hovered over the small tables strategically placed outside of each small restaurant. Eye catching canvas awnings shaded each store window. The scene was filled with pops of color, enhanced by beams of sunlight. It truly looked like a perfect photograph from a travel magazine.

Before we stepped off of the bus, Simeon shared with us that this was the place to enjoy lunch crepes and hard cider. With this information in mind, we headed out to explore the charming village.

We soon discovered that every restaurant served the infamous crepes and cider, so we selected an eating establishment, settled in at an outdoor wooden table, and placed our order. As we waited for our lunch to arrive, we snapped a few photos and recapped the highlights of our trip so far.

When the crepes materialized at our table, we were amazed by the size of these entrees. One crepe took up an entire dinner plate and resembled a large whole-wheat pancake. A bite revealed the rubbery texture of the crepe with melted cheese, diced ham, and vegetables hidden inside. We quickly decided to abandon the bland tasting crepe and focused on eating the filling. The cider was disappointing. Rather than being sparkling, it was more like a bitter beer, however we were simply grateful to have some form of liquid to quench our thirsts.

As we finished our lunch, a warm, gentle rain began to fall, so we donned our clear, plastic rain ponchos and popped up our umbrella. We used our remaining time to visit several small shops in search of souvenirs for our family members and friends. With time running out and our souvenir quest unsuccessful, we headed back to the bus empty handed.

Our guide greeted us with, "Did you have the crepes and cider?"

"Yes, we did," I replied, conveniently leaving out our opinions regarding the tastes of these lunch items.

The rain continued as we traveled to our last stop for the day, the resort town of Deauville, also known as The Parisian Riviera or The Queen of Norman Beaches. As the aliases imply, Deauville is a popular vacation spot for the international upper class. This was very apparent as we drove through the streets lined with expensive luxury cars. Our plastic rain ponchos purchased back home at our local Wal-Mart didn't seem to fit in with the waterproof, designer jackets most people were wearing. The clothing discrepancy didn't bother us. Our identities were clear. We were middle class tourists from America and proud of it!

Still wearing our rain ponchos, we unloaded our luggage from the bus and quickly checked into our hotel. Once situated in our room, we draped our dripping ponchos over two chairs and took the opportunity to call a friend in Colorado Springs to check on the status of the fire.

According to our friend Scott, the Waldo Canyon Fire had started on June 23rd approximately three miles northwest of Colorado Springs in the Pike National Forest. Erratic winds had caused the fire to spread rapidly to the east and south on a direct course toward Colorado Springs. Flames one hundred and fifty feet above the treetops had been reported by several firefighters. None of our friends had been asked to leave their homes. Our neighborhood was in a rural area to the north of Colorado Springs, known as the Black Forest, and it was not in any imminent danger. We ended the conversation by thanking Scott for taking the time to speak with us and vowing to pray for the people affected by the fire.

That day had certainly been filled with many questions about the relationship between mankind and nature. The gardens at Monet's home seemed to prove the theory that man and nature can coexist in a symbiotic relationship. The Cathedral at Rouen seemed to prove the theory that, despite nature's ruthless, destructive events, man can prevail through perseverance. There were lessons to be learned close to home as well.

We, like many Coloradans, had settled in areas so we could enjoy and appreciate the views, activities, and resources around us. In our quest to meet our wants and needs, we had cleared the land, forced the wildlife from their habitats, and exploited the natural resources. Nature had fought back with storms, dangerous weather conditions, and now a raging forest fire.

Once again the nagging questions arose in my gut. Why is there a constant battle between humans and nature? When we use the word nature, are we really referring to God? Is nature our friend or foe? Perhaps the answer to this question depends on how we treat nature, with appreciation and admiration, or as an entity to be controlled, managed, and exploited. Friend or foe, perhaps we will never know.

Chapter 21
Holy Ground

"Time will not dim the glory of their deeds."
These words were engraved in the wall of the
visitor's center at the Normandy American
Cemetery and Memorial. There was so much truth
in those words. Sixty-eight years after D-Day, we
were standing on the bluff above Omaha Beach
paying homage to the American soldiers who gave
their lives to save the lives of others during WW II.
Certainly their brave deeds were not lessened by the
passage of time; perhaps their deeds were even
intensified.

Our day had begun by loading onto the bus
before the first rays of the sunrise peeked over the
horizon. No one was late because we all knew it
was a special day. We were going to the beaches
where the allied forces landed on D-Day. As our
fellow travelers boarded the bus, many of them
stopped to ask us for an update on the fire in
Colorado Springs and the status of our home. Once
again, we were grateful for their concern and shared
what little information we had gathered.

As we drove through the French countryside, I
admired the fields of green crops, golden wheat,
perky sunflowers, and purple waves of lavender
plants. While Paris had a sophisticated,
metropolitan air, the French countryside had a
simplistic beauty.

Finally, when we caught a glimpse of the
Atlantic Ocean, we knew our destination was near.
As we pulled into the parking lot, we were

breathless with anticipation, but it was the scene before us that took breath away. Ten large sections of green grass were lined with perfectly manicured deciduous trees. Amidst all this natural beauty, were the precisely aligned headstones of white Lasa marble crosses, which marked the graves of nine thousand three hundred eighty-seven brave souls who lost their lives on D-Day, June 6, 1944.

Four people from our group had been chosen to raise the two American flags at the entrance of the cemetery. A middle-aged couple raised the first flag while the National Anthem echoed through the trees. A young boy and his grandmother raised the second flag while a trumpeter played "Taps." At last my long awaited goose bumps appeared, not because I had found the meaning in life, but because I knew I was standing on holy ground. Each year over one million people visit this spot. For some, it is a vacation destination, but for others it is a pilgrimage made to honor the brave men who gave their lives so that generations to come could live in freedom.

After the flag raising ceremony, we were given a generous amount of time to explore the area independently. Greg and I followed a path, which led down the bluff to Omaha Beach. Along the way, we stopped to explore several bunkers, which had been occupied by the German soldiers. These cave-like rooms had been dug into the hills and cliffs along the shoreline. The interiors of the bunkers were dark, cold, and damp. Bunk bed frames and iron stoves indicated that perhaps the soldiers lived in the bunkers guarding the beaches twenty-four hours a day, seven day a week.

The beach was stark and desolate. No rocks. No bushes. Not even a blade of grass. Only sand. I couldn't imagine being an American soldier disembarking from the landing craft, entering the chest deep water, wading to shore, only to find there was no cover for protection. The beach was riddled with hidden landmines, and German bullets filled the air. Fear must have been a factor in this situation, but was it overtaken by bravery? What was the motivation for these young men in order for them to look death squarely in the eye, yet continue on what many considered to be a suicide mission? It was a fact that many of them had been drafted into the armed forces and were simply following orders, but there was something beyond simply being obedient. I would like to think it had to do with our connections as humans, what I refer to as our "humanness." We have an almost innate need to connect with other people. In this case perhaps it had to do with standing up for what is right. People in Europe were being killed and tortured in horrible, unimaginable ways. It was not only wrong. It was evil.

"The world is a dangerous place to live, not because of the people who are evil, but because of the people who don't do anything about it." These words of wisdom were spoken by Albert Einstein. These brave souls were certainly willing to do something about stopping the spread of evil throughout the world, even to the point of sacrificing their own lives to save the lives of complete strangers, and to guarantee freedom for generations in the future. Truly, there are points on the timeline of history where the world is changed forever. June 6th, 1944, D-Day, is certainly one of those points. Perhaps knowing you were changing the course of history for the positive was a factor as well. The reasons why fear was replaced by courage and bravery could only be found in the minds and hearts of the souls who stormed the beaches on that fateful day. Many of those reasons perished along with the soldiers on the blood stained beaches of Normandy. Fortunately, many of those reasons survived along with the many soldiers who lived through that historical battle.

These reasons and stories of the soldiers who lived and died that day were found at the museum at the top of the bluff. There encased in glass display cases were the boots, uniforms, weapons, and personal belongings of many of the soldiers. Through printed stories and treasured photographs, we learned about their jobs, their families, their hopes and dreams, the people they loved, and their reasons for fighting. From their letters and journal entries, we felt their emotions from missing their families and loved ones, to the fear that crept into their lives on a daily basis. Even though they were physically gone, we could feel their presence in the rooms of the museum. We could feel their "humanness."

Although we could have easily spent the entire day at this site, our time was up so we headed back to the tour bus. I thought of this quote as we left the museum, "Evil is powerless if the good are unafraid." I silently said a prayer of thanksgiving to the brave souls who had given the ultimate sacrifice and faced their fears in order to change history by stopping the spread of evil throughout the world. Thank you, dear ones. Thank you.

On D-Day one hundred thirty thousand allied troops landed on five beaches. The American forces stormed the German strongholds on the Omaha and Utah Beaches. Canadian soldiers captured the Juno Beach, and the British secured Sword and Gold Beaches.

Our bus was now heading toward Gold Beach. Gold Beach didn't include a cemetery or museum like Omaha Beach, but it was impressive in a different way. Once Gold Beach was secured, the British began transporting floating, metal harbors across the English Channel. These structures were known as Mulberry harbors and were set up at Gold and Omaha Beaches. During WW II, many French harbors and ports were under German control. The harbors, which were abandoned by the Nazis, had been sabotaged, so the Mulberry harbors were a creative solution to the lack of Allied controlled harbors in Europe. This creative solution proved to be very successful. In the ten months the Mulberry harbors were operational at Gold beach, two million men, five hundred thousand vehicles, and four million tons of supplies were quickly transported into France.

Greg and I were surprised that several of the Mulberry harbors were still floating in the water. A few had washed up on the beach so we were able to inspect these structures up close. Granted they were covered with rust and barnacles, but they were spectacular, nonetheless. It wasn't the physical aspects of these metal constructions that were splendid as much as the creative, think outside of the box idea they represented. In times of necessity it is amazing what the human mind can imagine and turn into reality. Although we had studied WW II, Greg and I had never heard about these magnificent floating harbors. Once again we saw before us how man manipulated nature to fulfill his needs.

As we enjoyed our lunch on the towering deck of a restaurant on the beach, we imagined the hustle and bustle of ships unloading precious cargo each day. Gold Beach must have been a busy, pivotal stronghold for the Allied forces.

"On the Road Again" seemed to be our theme song for the day, as we boarded the bus. As we traveled to Mont Saint Michel, the colorful fields filled with a variety of vegetation became green pastures filled with sheep. The magic of Mont Saint Michel is that it is a gigantic stone structure built on an island. When the tide goes out, people can walk or use other forms of transportation to reach the island. When the tide comes in, Mont Saint Michel is completely surrounded by water. This seemed to be a clever way to use Mother Nature as a natural defense from enemies.

From our bus windows, the stone structure looked like an enormous castle from a fairy tale. Rather than being a domicile for royalty, it was an abbey occupied by monks and nuns during most of its existence. The first small buildings were erected on the island in the early 700s. These were expanded until the end of the 16th century with the end result being the massive structure we saw before us.

Suddenly, it was the end of the road for us. Literally the road ended, and there was nothing but a huge expanse of sand between the island and us. We departed our tour bus, divided into small groups, and loaded into white vans. When the vans could no longer continue, we traversed the remaining distance to the island on foot.

Mont Saint Michel consisted of four layers. Outside of the stone walls was the housing for the fishermen and farmers. Inside the walls, the next layer looked like a city street with many shops as well as the homes of the fifty people who currently lived and worked at Mount Saint Michel permanently. A hike up several flights of steep, stone steps led us to The Great Halls. These massive, empty, cave-like rooms were used for large numbers of people to gather. More flights of steps took us a large grassy open area surrounded by flower and vegetable plants. On the outskirts of this beautiful natural area, were the places where the monks and nuns lived. Finally, on the very top layer, was a statue of the namesake of the entire island, Michael the Archangel. It seemed quite fitting for the statue to be at the highest point on the island, as close to heaven as humanly possible.

The day's sites and events had added data to a hypothesis that was forming in my mind. Throughout history the human race has manipulated nature to meet the needs of humanity. The floating harbors at the beaches of Normandy were an example. The use of the tides as protection at Mont Saint Michel were another. On a personal level, I thought of my battle against cancer. Was it another example of human beings clashing against nature? Were the surgery, radiation treatments, and medication my way of making nature conform to my needs?

On another level, I wondered if the forest fire raging near our home was nature's way of fighting back? It seemed as if this trip which I had deemed to be a quest for answers, had only resulted in even more questions. As we prepared to leave Mont Saint Michel, I decided to squelch these questions for the time being. Perhaps by letting them simmer for a while, I could come closer to finding the answers.

Even though descending down the steps was much easier than the climb, we were exhausted from the day's events. Certainly, the day had began and ended on holy ground. Mont Saint Michel, a home and sanctuary for monks and nuns, had been baptized for centuries by the rising and falling waters of the tides. The D-Day beaches had been consecrated by not only the blood of thousands of soldiers, but also by their valor and bravery. Truly, it was a day to remember . . . a day spent on holy ground.

Normandy American Cemetery

Chapter 22
Burned Pizza and Lost Souls

"Is your home still okay?" This was the question everyone asked us as they boarded the bus the next morning.

"Yes, our house is still okay," we replied each time. "Thank you for asking."

We had called our friend and neighbor, Tim, the previous evening to get on update on the fire and the status of our neighborhood. According to Tim, eleven thousand people had been evacuated from the mountain town of Woodland Park and the western sections of Colorado Springs. Due to the dry terrain, high temperatures, and erratic winds, the fire was at zero percent containment. Fire crews from every city and small town in the area had been called in to help, as well as a crew from Peterson Air Force base in Colorado Springs and many crews from bordering states. At this point in time, our neighborhood was not on evacuation alert. Once again we said prayers of gratitude but also prayers of intercession asking for God's mercy to save people and their homes that were in harm's way. We tucked the information about the fire in the back of our minds, so we could face the new day with a positive attitude.

Our first tour stop was the fortified, seaside city of Saint Malo. We enjoyed the cobblestone streets of this walled city, soaked in the ocean views, and marveled at the tales of local history.

Throughout history, the city had often been attacked so the residents simply built a wall around it. Saint Malo was known as the home of many

pirates who were sanctioned by the King.
Eventually, these pirates were asked by the King to
become the first French Navy. This request seemed
logical at the time since the pirates had ships and
knew how to sail them. After a brief tour of the
city's cathedral and a walk along the city's walls to
view the ocean, we boarded the tour bus and
continued on our journey until we reached the city of
Rennes.

In this city famous for its medieval half-timbered
buildings, we were given a large block of time to
explore the local shops and to eat lunch. We decided
to dine first and use our remaining time to shop.
Unfortunately in life, sometimes a wrench is thrown
into the machinery of your best-laid plans.

We found a quaint restaurant, which appeared to
be somewhat busy. We took this as a good sign. If
so many people had decided to dine there then the
food must be good. We made our way up to the
second floor since the bottom level was packed. We
quickly ordered drinks and a pizza to share. Our
drinks arrived and were refilled several times, but the
pizza hadn't appeared despite our continual requests
for the waiter to check on it.

The bewitching hour, otherwise known as the
time we needed to be back at the bus, was drawing
near. We had resigned ourselves to the fact that we
had enjoyed a liquid lunch consisting of our
beverages, when our pizza finally showed up at our
table. It was smokin'. Not in the sense that it was
"smokin' good," but in the literal sense of the word.
The pizza was so burned that smoke was rising from
the blackened crust. Our lunch was one step above a

pile of ashes. We had no time to complain or ask for another pizza, so we reluctantly washed down the toppings with our room temperature drinks.

Disappointed with our meal, and by the fact we didn't have any time to explore the shops, we scurried back to our designated meeting spot. We all arrived at the bus around the same time. As we waited in line to board, we found out that many of our fellow travelers had experienced similar lunch scenarios at a variety of eating establishments. Long wait times and substandard food seemed to be the common factors in our lunchtime adventures.

After our guide did a quick headcount, he informed us that two people were missing. Much to our surprise, it wasn't the normal tardy couple. It was the two young ladies from South Korea. We were all concerned because this was so unlike them. They were always very punctual. Simeon, our tour guide, asked if any of us had seen them during our allotted time in the city. One couple had seen them in a shop, but that was it.

Simeon glanced at his watch, had a short conversation with the driver, then sat down in his seat to wait. It was probably a few minutes, but it seemed like an eternity before he stood up and addressed us with the microphone.

"I'm going to go search for our fellow travelers, but I would like all of you to stay on the bus. I assure you that the young ladies will be fine, but you must promise me to stay on the bus." With that he departed and disappeared into the cobblestone streets.

During the extended time Simeon was gone, a sense of panic and concern permeated the interior of the bus. Instead of worrying, I decided to use the time for a positive purpose and began praying for the safety of the missing young women. About the time when several people were going to form their own search party, someone shouted, "I see them!" When we looked in the directions of the voice, we all saw Simeon and the two young women walking toward the bus.

In a few short minutes, the young ladies were climbing aboard followed by our guide. When the young women reached the landing by the driver, we all began to applaud.

"We are so sorry. We got lost," one of the women explained.

"We will sing any song you want," the other added.

One of the women from the boisterous group in the back of the bus immediately declared herself the spokeswoman for all of us. "Honey, forget the song," she exclaimed in her beautiful southern accent. " We are just glad you 'all are safe!" The bus exploded with applause again.

The young ladies plopped down in their seats with a sigh of relief. Once they were situated, the woman sitting behind them reached through the seats, giving them each a tender squeeze on the shoulder as she gently uttered, "We are glad you are safe."

Suddenly Simeon was at the front of the bus with the microphone in hand.

"I want to thank all of you for your patience and understanding, " he began. "We are all glad that the

lost have been found. During the search, I developed
a plan so this won't happen again. When we leave
the bus, I would like each of you to take a photo of
the nearest street sign. If you become lost then you
can show the photo to someone who can give you
directions. Does that sound like a good plan to
everybody?"

We all agreed it was a good plan, but I couldn't
help thinking that maybe we should have been doing
this throughout the entire trip. It also might have
been a good idea for each of us to put the tour
guide's phone number into our cell phones. A
simple phone call or digital photo of your location
could be invaluable.

With all of our fellow travelers finally aboard,
we traveled down the highway to our next
destination, which was a winery in the French
countryside. How ironic. After what we'd been
through, I was certain we could all appreciate a stiff
drink.

Chapter 23
Cherished Thinking

Calls to several of our friends in Colorado Springs that evening, revealed that June 26th was another day that the fire advanced at a rapid pace. That day Colorado Springs had a record high temperature of one hundred and one degrees. The sixty-five mile an hour winds from the west had pushed the fire toward the city at a rate of two miles per hour. Three hundred forty-six homes in the western neighborhoods of Colorado Springs had burned to the ground. To add fuel to the fire, no rain was in the forecast. Our home wasn't in the path of the fire although a quick change in the direction of the wind could instantly change that. We were thankful our friends and neighbors were safe for the time being.

All we could do was pray. Pray for the protection of our home, the well-being of our friends, and the safety of the residents of Colorado Springs. We also prayed for the brave firefighters who were risking their lives to control and hopefully stop the destructive fire. Once again, we shared what little news we knew about the fire with our fellow travelers as they voiced their concern to us before settling into their seats on the bus the next morning.

That day's docket of adventures included a visit to The Chateau de Chenonceau. Throughout history, the chateau had several owners and admirers. Many French kings, their queens, and their mistresses considered the castle a rural retreat secluded from the hustle and bustle of Paris. The area offered those who visited the opportunity to rest, relax, and revitalize.

After a myriad of owners, the Menier family, famous for their chocolate business, bought the chateau in 1913. After the castle was bombed during WW II, the Menier family financed the chateau's restoration in 1951. Today, the family runs the chateau Chenonceau as a business. In addition to daily tours, the grounds and castle can be rented for large-scale business and social events such as conferences, weddings, and galas.

The road leading to the chateau cut through a magical wooded area of white-barked trees. Ferns and moss covered the forest floor like a lush, green carpet. Intermittent beams of sunlight pierced the thick canopy of branches and leaves. Suddenly, the magical spell of the forest was broken as we drove out of the trees and into a beautiful grassy meadow. It was as if we had been transported into a fairy tale world, complete with a castle looming in the distance. The white exterior and blue roofs were reminiscent of the castles at Disney World or Disneyland. Only this castle was much larger and more magnificent.

Once we departed from the bus and walked closer to the exquisite structure, I almost expected to see Rapunzel's glorious locks cascading from one of the tower windows, or for Cinderella to greet us at the door dressed in her ball gown and glass slippers. Alas, no princess appeared, but what we saw before us was just as beautiful.

The chateau was built over the river utilizing several stone pillars and arches so the water flowed under the castle. A mirror image of the structure was reflected in the water. Trees framed the castle. Perfectly manicured gardens flanked both sides of the estate. The Mistress Garden greeted visitors with bursts of colors including red, white and pink roses, and waves of lavender plants. The Queen's Garden consisted of many shades of green including bushes trimmed to create intricate mazes. Fountains, sculptures, and benches adorned both gardens and added to the inviting feel of the environment. The property also included an enormous, exquisitely maintained vegetable garden. The scene seemed to portray a symbiotic relationship between humans and nature.

The interior of the chateau was just as appealing as the exterior. Although it was regal and classic, it was bright, charming, and cheerful. Black and white tiles covered the floors. Some walls were white, while others where covered with elaborate textured wallpaper. Flowers from the estate's gardens were displayed in beautiful arrangements throughout the castle. Paintings in golden frames adorned the massive walls. Stunning tapestries used for window coverings and upholstery added to the grandeur and opulence. Even though the chateau had electricity, many of the rooms were illuminated with lanterns and candles. The hinged windows were open to let in the natural light along with the cool, calming breeze and the hypnotic sound of the river below.

We meandered through the rooms of the castle, drinking in its culture and ambiance. The chapel greeted us with colorful beams of light filtering through the stained glass windows. Banquet and ballrooms reminded us of the need to socialize with others. Elaborate bedrooms furnished with massive fireplaces, canopy beds, lavish fabrics and tapestries, and oil paintings, reminded us of our need for rest. One particular room showcased the history of the chateau with blueprints, sketches, drawings, and paintings of the spectacular structure as it evolved through time.

Of course, the heart of any home is the kitchen. The same was true of the chateau. Located in the lower level, the kitchen was a mixture of functionality and character. Shiny copper pots and pans hung from the ceiling like magnificent chandeliers. Artistic wall displays of knives and cutlery added flare to the decor. Small planters of herbs adorned the rustic wooden table adding color and inviting aromas. A large black cauldron hung in the fireplace, and gray ashes covered the hearth as if a meal had just been prepared.

While the kitchen was inviting, the most exciting room in the castle was the salon. Throughout history, the Chateau Chenonceau attracted royalty, leaders, and many great thinkers. Writers, naturalists, playwrights, musicians, philosophers, composers, and inventors flocked to this paradise in the French countryside to create, wonder, ponder, think, and share ideas. The salon was a long hallway stretching over the river with its windows open to let in the sunlight and allowing the breeze to flow through this hallowed corridor. Paintings and sketches created by famous artists hung from the walls. Display cases held pieces of music scribbled on paper by well-known composers. There were hand written notes of philosophers, as well as sketches and models of inventions. Quotes were sprinkled throughout the area like magical glitter of thoughts and ideas. It was clear from the contents of this historical shrine that thinking was valued, honored, and cherished.

I felt the need to capture a few of these thoughts and ideas, which so eloquently summarized my philosophy of education and life, so I retrieved a notepad from my backpack.

"Firstly, know well that it is rarely up to you to suggest to him what he should learn; it is for him to desire, to seek, to find; for you to put it within his reach, to skillfully allow his desire to be born and to provide him with the means to satisfy it." These delicious words were "mind candy" to my soul for this quote expressed the very essence of education and our roles as teachers.

I was contemplating these words and thoughts as if suspended in time, when Greg's voice beckoned me back to reality. It was time to go. Needless to say, I could have spent the entire day lost in the magic of the chateau, but it wasn't meant to be. As we exited the salon, another quote caught my eye. "Dare I share the greatest secret? It is not to gain time but to lose it." That was the true spirit of the chateau, to lose oneself in time.

We had spent the morning at the Chateau Chenonceau, and now we were off to spend the afternoon at the Chateau d' Amboise. While the Chateau d' Amboise was just as massive and beautiful as Chenonceau, it didn't have the same warmth and charm. It had been confiscated by the royal family in the 15th century, rebuilt, and soon became a favorite residence of many French monarchs. The chateau fell into disrepair during the 16th century. It followed a pattern of disrepair and reconstruction for many years, and at one time, it even served as a prison.

We enjoyed the tour of the interior of the chateau with its enormous rooms, marble floors, grand gold-framed paintings, crystal chandeliers, and elegant sculptures, but it was the simple Chapel of Saint Hubert built in the garden area away from the chateau that stole our hearts. This understated chapel is the final resting place of Leonardo Da Vinci. A floor-level marble stone with a medal medallion relief portrait, and his named etched on the bottom of the stone, marks the grave of one of the most diversely talented human beings to have ever walked the face of the earth.

Leonardo Da Vinci was known as a polymath who lived during the Renaissance era. A polymath is a person with wide-ranging knowledge and learning who excels across a diverse range of areas. This was certainly true of Da Vinci. He excelled in the arts and was a master at drawing, painting, and sculpting. He composed music and wrote pieces of literature. He was an outstanding scientist making discoveries and hypothesis in astronomy, paleontology, geology, botany, and anatomy. He passionately delved into mathematics by exploring architecture and engineering. He was an inventor who could conceptualize ideas that wouldn't become a reality until centuries later. He sketched ideas for airplanes, helicopters, and parachutes. He toyed with the ideas of solar power, models of the solar systems, and sketches of his understanding of the human anatomy. It has been said that Leonardo Da Vinci not only *thought* outside of the box, but he *saw* outside of the box.

Although Da Vinci was Italian, King Francis I invited him to France in December 1515 so Leonardo could share his knowledge and skills. Leonardo accepted the invitation, living and working in the nearby Clos Luce', which was connected to the Chateau d' Amboise by a series of underground passages. Throughout his stay in France, Da Vinci's health weakened. Eventually, he suffered a series of several strokes and died on May 2, 1519 at the age of sixty-seven.

Standing at the gravesite of one of the most diversely intelligent and creative people to have ever lived, I felt proud to be a teacher. I was proud that I valued thinking, intelligence, diversity, and creativity. Not only did I value these concepts, but I had devoted my professional life to nurturing these characteristics in others. This was my calling, my passion, my life. As a teacher being in the "presence" of one of the greatest minds to have ever existed was not only surreal, but exciting and invigorating. I felt one step closer to finding the meaning in my life that I was so desperately searching for.

Initially, the draw of the chateaus we had explored that day were physical. The massive size of the structures, the incredible engineering concepts, and the beauty of the architecture were astounding and impressive. But the true magic and mystic of these palaces were intangible. The ideas and beliefs these places represented intrigued me. Within these time periods, within these hallowed environments, thinking was encouraged, nurtured, and cherished. In my world, in my time period, money and fame were valued. Somehow knowing I cherished thinking seemed to put me at peace. It wasn't the answer I was looking for, but at this moment in time, it seemed to be enough.

Chateau Chenonceau

Chapter 24
Au Revoir

Today had a bittersweet essence to it. It would be our last day with our tour group. I would miss the new friends we had made. I would miss our daily adventures, which transported us into realms of the past. I would miss Simeon, our informative, jovial tour guide. I would even miss the terminally tardy couple who nonchalantly sang a variety of songs on a daily basis as a punishment for not being punctual.

For the last time, we shared the status of our home and an update on the wildfire's progress toward Colorado Springs with our fellow travelers as they entered the tour bus. By this time, thirty thousand people had been evacuated due to the fire. Firefighters from across Colorado and bordering states had been called in to help battle the blaze. The brave heroes had been housed at local schools, sleeping on cots in gyms and showering in the locker rooms. Crowds of people gathered at the schools, greeting the firefighters with banners, signs, and cheers expressing their gratitude for these unsung heroes who came to save homes, businesses, and lives. A black cloud of smoke and ash had rumbled over Pikes Peak into the city of Colorado Springs, creating a nighttime atmosphere even though it was the middle of the day. Many residents had to be hospitalized due to breathing problems caused by the smoke. Embers carried by the gusting winds had started several smaller fires up to a quarter of a mile away. Yet the exhausted firefighters continued to battle on, and our home was still safe.

Upon departing the bus in the streets of Blois, our tour guide, Simeon, suggested we take a group photo since it was our last day together. We thought this was a terrific idea, so we lined our cameras on the surface of the street in from of him. He patiently and carefully took a photo with each camera, then returned it to the surface of the street. After the photo shoot, we reclaimed our cameras and thanked Simeon for capturing the important moment.

We enjoyed the colorful hanging baskets of flowers that lined the cobblestone streets, as we made our way to the picturesque cathedral at the center of the city. After exploring the interior, we boarded the bus in order to venture to the castle at Blois, which had been the residence for many members of the royal families throughout several centuries. Although this chateau contained five hundred sixty-four rooms, only a few were available for the public to view. There were several references made to Joan of Arc because she had visited the castle in order to be blessed before she defeated the English at the battle of Orleans. By this time in our trip, we had seen so many chapels, churches, cathedrals, and castles that we had simply overdosed on seeing historical architecture. We were anxious to return to Paris that afternoon, where many of us had scheduled optional excursions. Our excursion was the Louvre, my main reason for wanting to visit France in the first place.

As the tour bus came to a stop in front of the Louvre, I was sitting on the edge of my seat anxiously waiting for my turn to enter the aisle and disembark from the bus. Once off the bus, we joined the massive line to purchase our tickets and to obtain our audio tour. As we entered the museum, we became part of the mass of humanity. Our bodies were shoulder to shoulder with complete strangers. We moved through the exhibits as a gigantic mass of human beings, with multiple heads and hundreds of legs. No one spoke. Everyone had on headphones, which allowed each person to hear the audio tour in the language of his or her choice. The people in the mob would stop periodically to raise their cameras above their heads to snap a few photos.

The first exhibit was of ancient statues, all of which were naked, and many were missing heads or limbs. *Not what I had expected.* From there, the mob of sweating human flesh moved on to a gallery of gigantic gold-framed paintings. We had seen many similar pieces of art at the myriad of castles we had toured throughout the week, so we were unimpressed. Finally, the hall-like gallery opened up into a large room. On the wall, many yards in front of us, was the Mona Lisa. Hundreds of cameras were hoisted into the air. The sound of camera shudders clicking and bursts of light from the flashes filled the room.

My first response was . . . *that's it? What a disappointment.* The painting was small, very small. I had expected it to be massive, huge, in your face. It was enclosed in a clear case, so there was no way to look at the brushstrokes or to admire Da Vinci's technique.

Of course, I had seen pictures of the Mona Lisa, but I had expected when I saw it in person, there would be something magical about the face of this famous woman. She was just a woman. She wasn't beautiful. She was plain at best. Her expression wasn't mysterious, as I had anticipated. It was nothingness. I looked at Greg and shrugged my shoulders as an expression of my disappointment. The look on his face suggested he was feeling the same way.

As the saying goes, "When in Rome, do as the Romans do," but in this case it was, "When in France, do as the French do." So I raised my camera over my head and took a photo of the Mona Lisa. Before I knew it, the mob of humanity was moving on to the next exhibit. We traveled as a mass through several galleries, admiring the art from what seemed like the beginning of time to the present. Finally, we ended in what appeared to be the basement, which was filled with Egyptian artifacts. Many people had dropped out of the tour, so we could move without touching the people next to us. Without the stress of being crushed by other human beings, I enjoyed this exhibit a little more than the previous ones.

With the tour completed, we returned our headphones and audio equipment before entering an open courtyard surrounded by shops. We took this opportunity to speak to each other.

"What did you think?" Greg asked.

"That was the most disappointing thing I have ever experienced," I confessed.

"Yeah, that's how I felt, too," he shared. "I just wanted to know if you had a different take on it. Can you believe the size of the Mona Lisa?" he added, and then we both laughed. We purchased a couple of French pastries and beverages, and continued our conversation while we enjoyed our delicious treats.

Since we hadn't purchased any gifts for our friends and family members, we decided to use our remaining time to explore the shops on the streets of Paris. We peered into the windows of many quaint storefronts, but found nothing that seemed to beckon us inside. Finally, as the last beams of sunlight illuminated the horizon, we made our way down a narrow, cobblestone alley. As night engulfed twilight, we entered a cozy, well-lit shop

At first I thought the place was deserted, when suddenly a short, stout, gray-haired man appeared beside me.

"Bonsoir, madame."

"Bonsoir, monsieur."

A closer look at the gentleman revealed he was dressed in a crisp, white, button down shirt and belted, dark, dress pants. Somehow he looked vaguely familiar. Then it hit me! *Chef Boyardee.* He looked like Chef Boyardee without the hat.

In broken English delightfully sprinkled with a French accent, he explained he was the owner of the establishment and offered his assistance. In a mixture of English and broken French, I explained I was looking for gifts for our friends and family members. He immediately escorted me to a wall covered with scarves. He whisked his arm across the display with a flourish and added, "Enjoy," then he returned to his post at the checkout counter.

Perfect. I was looking for something functional, yet stylish, and I wouldn't have to worry about purchasing the correct sizes. Scarves were truly the ultimate fashion statement in France. Everyone wore them, men and women. It would be fun to bring back a little bit of French culture to share with our loved ones. I had several scarves draped over my arm when the gentleman appeared by my side.

"Let me take those for you so it will be easier for you to shop," he insisted as he removed the items from my arm. "Perhaps you would like to look at these?" he added as he again whisked his arm in a dramatic gesture toward the display table behind me.

There I found an array of jewelry and a variety of souvenirs. I selected several bracelets, an Eiffel Tower snow globe (which our daughter had requested), and a billfold for our son. With our selections complete, we headed to the checkout counter. At the counter, Greg and I did a quick inventory, touching each item while simultaneously saying the name of the person for who it was intended. We didn't want to forget anyone.

"That should do it," I informed the shopkeeper, indicating I was ready to complete our business transaction.

"Nothing for you, madame?" he questioned.

"Oh, no," was my response. "I am just shopping for my friends, and thanks to you, I am going to be able to give them such beautiful gifts."

"Such a generous lady needs something for herself," he insisted. I was thinking he was trying to make one more sale.

"No, this trip is my gift," I explained.

He smiled at me then he walked over to the wall of scarves where he selected one, then walked back to the counter. He stopped in front of me and held out the scarf.

"For you," he said. "A beautiful gift for a beautiful lady."

"Oh, no. I can't accept such an extravagant gift," I told him.

"I insist," he said as he flashed his charming smile.

I was so touched by his thoughtful gesture that I was momentarily speechless. I snapped myself out of the trance of gratitude and whispered, "Merci beaucoup! (thank you very much) May I give you a hug?"

"Of course," he chuckled as he outstretched his arms to receive the embrace. I gave him a real hug, not just a pat on the back. I wanted to express my appreciation, not only for the elegant scarf, but also for his beautiful gesture of kindness.

I handed him my credit card, then wrapped the gorgeous scarf around my neck. Instantly, I felt a surge of French confidence pulse through me. Perhaps my newfound friend had given me more than just a scarf.

As we exited the shop into the darkness of the alley, I turned back for one more glance at the gentleman's glowing face.

Merci beaucoup," I told him one last time. "Au revoir."

"Au revoir, madame." Then he waved good-bye.

Chapter 25
The Definition of a Masterpiece

"Where's Landon?" When our son Landon was a toddler, he would ask this whenever he played with his jack-in-the-box. Both of our children were adopted and were born in the Philippines. In both cases, once we were matched, we were sent a photograph of each child, and we were allowed to send a photo of us along with a toy to the orphanage. After each match was made, it was several months before we could travel to the Philippines to meet our children, so the photos played a significant role in the development of our family.

After we were matched with Sierra, we sent her an adorable rag doll with dark hair and brown eyes along with a photograph of Greg and me. When we were matched with Landon, I had what I thought was a stroke of genius. I purchased a jack-in-the-box. I added a photo of Greg, Sierra, and me sitting on the lawn with our home in the background. Each time the clown from inside the musical box popped out, he was holding the photo of Landon's new family and home.

When Landon first joined our family, he was just learning to walk and wasn't talking yet. He loved playing with his jack-in-the-box, but it was clear he made no connection between us, and the people in the photo that popped out of his favorite toy. When the clown jumped out of the box holding the picture, I would point at each family member in the

213

photo then simultaneously point at the actual person in the room.

As Landon's first year with us progressed, so did his language and cognitive skills. Soon his language skills allowed him to ask the inevitable question, "Where's Landon?" when the clown popped out holding the family photo. Landon wanted to know why he wasn't in the family picture. Each time he asked, I would attempt to explain that at the time the photo was taken, he didn't live with us yet. He lived in a house in the Philippines, while we lived in our house in Colorado.

I knew that Landon wasn't developmentally ready to understand this concept, but I also knew that the repetition of what I was telling him would one day help him understand. He just had to be ready, and until he was ready, I had to be patient and keep explaining it to him.

Finally, after years of repetition, the day arrived when Landon understood why he wasn't in the jack-in-the-box family photo. We were standing in front of the world map in his room. When he asked, "Where's Landon?"

I explained, "Landon was here." Then I pointed to the Philippines on the map. "Mom, Dad, and Sierra were here," I added as I pointed to Colorado. "Sierra stayed with Grandma in Colorado so Mom and Dad could fly on an airplane to the Philippines to get Landon." I then moved my fingers across the map from Colorado to the Philippines. "Then Landon came back to Colorado on the airplane with Mom and Dad to live forever." I moved my fingers across the map again until I touched the outline of Colorado.

A giant smile spread across Landon's face. He clapped his hands and squealed with delight. As a teacher, I called this a "light bulb moment." It is when a child suddenly understands a concept. This situation with Landon reminded me of the many times God had tried to teach me a lesson or reveal something to me. He was always so patient in these circumstances, repeating His message over and over until I was developmentally ready to understand it.

I didn't know it at the time, but I was about to have a light bulb moment regarding a lesson God had been trying to teach me throughout my entire life.

On the day of our departure from France, Greg and I had taken the bus to the airport in Paris early in the morning. Once the plane was in the air, Greg quickly drifted off to sleep, and I was left alone with my thoughts.

I had made the trip to France with a very specific purpose in mind. I wanted to desperately find meaning in my life. If God saw fit to save my life from cancer, then I felt I should find a worthy purpose for it. For some strange reason, I thought I would find a purpose for my life at the Louvre. Somehow, I thought the answer to my quest was hidden in the sculptures and paintings at this world-renowned museum. If the great masters and thinkers of all time felt something was important enough to capture in a piece of art, then certainly those ideas and concepts must be paramount in my understanding of life.

But our experience at the Louvre had been disappointing. It was more than just the small size of the Mona Lisa. It was more than the collection of headless, limbless, naked sculptures. Granted, the masterpieces portrayed love, passion, sorrow, betrayal, anger, and joy, basically the entire spectrum of human emotions. But the haunting question for me was why would people from around the world visit the Louvre to simply view these emotions encapsulated in a piece of artwork, when each of us can actually experience these emotions in our everyday lives? To me, it was the equivalent of looking at a painting of an apple or actually eating an apple. There is no comparison.

Other thoughts kept popping into my mind. Who decides what is a masterpiece? Who decides what is worthy to put into the Louvre? In other words, who was the judge and jury concerning whether a piece of art truly reflected the meaning of life? I felt overwhelmed by all of these questions. Had our trip to France been a total waste of time?

I closed my eyes, cleared my mind of all thoughts, then in peaceful serenity I let my mind wander to where it wanted to go. It was here, a step or two beyond consciousness, that I often found the answers to my questions. It was here that God often spoke to me.

Memories of our trip began to flood into my mind like a series of colorful video clips. Visions of the elaborate structures of the Notre Dame Cathedral and the Palace at Versailles filtered into my imagination. These two excursions cemented something in my mind that I already knew. People are more important than things. Plain and simple. No discussion. That was it for me.

The smiling face of the young gentleman who gave us directions when we were lost in the streets of Paris appeared before me. He seemed to glow with pride at his ability to help two wayward strangers. He appeared to empathize with our fear of being lost in unfamiliar territory. There were so many emotions in that situation-our fear, his pride, empathy. While it is true that people are more important than things, what is it about people that make them so magical? It's our emotions.

Laughter is such a beautiful expression of the emotion of happiness. Laughter is what I remembered about our interaction with the waiter at the restaurant we dined at during our first night in Paris. Although we didn't share the same language, we communicated through other means including gestures, facial expressions, and of course, laughter. Satisfaction, gratitude, and happiness were emotions we communicated through that evening encounter. It was obvious my understanding was growing and building. People are more important than things. Emotions are what make people magical. Emotions must be communicated in order to be appreciated, but they can be communicated in many different ways.

A wonderful warmth spread throughout my entire being as I fondly remembered our fellow travelers. Each day, they boarded our tour bus and thoughtfully voiced their concern for our family, friends, and home, which were all in the path of dangerous wildfire. Their empathy quickly turned these mere strangers into cherished friends. By sharing emotions, we built relationships with our traveling companions. A relationship is like a bridge that emotions travel across from one person to another and back. The more emotions are shared, the stronger that bridge or relationship becomes.

My mind drifted to the day the two young women from South Korea were lost. Up until that day, the two of them kept to themselves, never interacting with the rest of our travel group. I simply thought they were shy, but once they realized how much all of us cared about them, they seemed to blossom into new people. Our tour guide had cared enough about them to go out into the streets to search for them. When they entered the bus, our applause and verbal sentiments regarding their safety were expressions of our care and concern. From that day on, the two young women spoke with us, joked, laughed, and shared tidbits about their lives. This situation offered an important lesson to be learned. On a daily basis people surround us, but if we don't interact with each other, we can never build relationships. I was beginning to understand the sweet spot in life, which is interacting with others to share emotions and eventually build relationships.

The sound of the waves lapping up on the shores of Omaha Beach floated through my imagination. The word sacrifice came to mind. The simplest definition of the word sacrifice is to give something up in return for something else. We all know the soldiers on the beaches of Normandy sacrificed more than just their physical bodies. They sacrificed their lives, which meant they gave up their ability to feel physically and emotionally. They gave up the ability to experience life, to love, to live. What did they receive in exchange for this sacrifice? They gave the people who were dominated, suppressed, and exploited by the Nazis, the ability to experience life and to live in freedom. Their sacrifices reached beyond the war-torn world of the 1940s and into the future. The men who stormed the beaches of Normandy had to be filled with emotions on that fateful day. Fear, uncertainty, bravery, and conviction were probably just a few of the emotions pulsating through their beings. Decades later, as visitors came to this hallowed ground to remember the sacrifices that were made, people felt the emotions of sorrow, wonder, indebtedness, and gratitude. The sacrifices made during WWII were truly an exchange of emotions, which created a relationship, which reached across generations and transcended time.

Yes, there is no doubt that emotions are intense, deep, life changing, and powerful, yet intangible, and ambiguous. So much so, that since the beginning of time, people have tried to make these concepts tangible by expressing them through art. You can't frame happiness or capture love in a jar, but you can see these emotions expressed in a painting, sculpture, book, play, or song.

To capture life, its emotions, its relationships, its ups and downs, its turmoil and tribulations was the goal of the thinkers and scholars who congregated at the Chateau of Chenonceau. These incredible people were intelligent enough to know that a math formula or a science theory may express a component of life. A song, book, or poem may express life's emotions, but these physical expressions of life do not originate from external sources. They originate from deep within the minds, souls, and imaginations of human beings. Where do people's minds, souls, and imaginations originate? God.

As an educator, I realize all good learning is circular in nature. Usually a learner processes thoughts only to find herself in the end at the very place where she began. In the beginning of my thought process, I had questioned what constitutes a masterpiece, and who decides what is a masterpiece? The most concise definition of a masterpiece is a work of outstanding artistry, skill, and workmanship. I think most people would agree the pieces of art at the Louvre are considered to be the world's greatest masterpieces, yet I felt the need to look beyond the confines of the walls of a mere museum, even beyond the physical aspects of art. I was thinking of living, breathing, changing forms of art. People. If a masterpiece is defined as a work of outstanding artistry, skill, and workmanship, then human beings are the perfect example of this definition. If we are the masterpieces, then God is the artist.

I had expected my search for meaning in life to end with an "ah ha" moment at the Louvre, but instead I realized our trip through France had been a process with a series of steps that led me to new knowledge, intellect, and understanding. Although God had been explaining these concepts to me throughout my entire life, I wasn't able to fully understand what He was revealing to me until I was developmentally ready, until this very moment in time while flying over the Atlantic Ocean.

I thought about the similarities between Landon's learning and my learning. The learning was a process with a series of hierarchical steps. It took time to travel thoughtfully through these steps. The learning required patience, repetition, and understanding on the part of the teacher. It required that the student was developmentally ready and willing to accept the new learning.

Each experience in France had taught me a lesson, and each lesson was a building block to a greater understanding. The understanding began with the basic realization that people are more important than things. It grew to include the fact that emotions make people unique, valuable, and magical. We need to interact with each other in order to share emotions. When we share emotions, we create relationships. We can create relationships that transcend generations and even time. Throughout history, members of the human race have struggled with expressing intangible emotions in the tangible forms of art. In the end, we must realize that we, human beings, are the ultimate, living, breathing masterpieces created by God, the ultimate artist.

My journey through this extensive thinking was exhausting yet exhilarating. My eyes fluttered open. I was anxious to share my newfound knowledge with someone! I looked over at my sleeping husband. He was not an option. I didn't know anyone else on the plane. *Are you kidding me?* At last, I had found the "holy grail," and I had no one to share my enlightenment with. *So much for sharing emotions and building relationships.*

I eased my body back into the comfort of the seat, closed my eyes, and waited for slumber to overtake my now peaceful mind. I found contentment in my "light bulb moment," but as we all know, in order to show mastery of new concepts, the learner must be tested. I didn't realize it at the time, but the testing of my newfound knowledge was lurking in the near future.

Chapter 26
A Test of Hope

Our scheduled stop in Montreal, Canada, lasted a bit longer than we had anticipated. Mechanical repairs needed to be made on the heating and cooling system that regulated the temperature of the plane's cabin. At first, we were told the repairs were minor and wouldn't take long, so we were instructed to stay on board in our seats. Over an hour later, the passengers were impatient, uncomfortable, dripping with sweat, and hovering on the verge of mutiny. An executive decision was made to allow everyone to disembark from the plane. We, like the majority of the passengers, headed to the nearest airport restaurant to purchase glasses of cold, refreshing sodas.

As I swiped the icy side of the plastic cup across my forehead, I admitted to Greg, "I never thought I would be this happy about having ice in my drink."

Ice had been a rare commodity in France. In fact, we were never served ice the entire time we were there. When we requested it, people looked at us like we were aliens from another planet.

"I agree," Greg added. "You had better chug that stuff. I think they just called our flight." He was right so we slammed our drinks and headed back to the plane.

Our extended layover at the Montreal airport put us behind schedule. Fortunately, we had left our car at the Denver airport, so we didn't have to worry about someone picking us up. Unfortunately, the delay put us at the prime time for the daily

223

afternoon thunderstorms that occur in Colorado during the spring and summer months. Sure enough, the closer we got to Denver the more turbulence we encountered. Before we knew it, the fasten your seat belt signs were on and the cabin lights were off. The plane seemed to plummet and soar through the sky like a car on a roller coaster track. A glance outside the window revealed colossal, black thunderclouds that churned and rolled as if they were terrifying monsters attempting to take control of the atmosphere. I quickly closed the window shade for fear the view outside would only heighten my level of terror. I glanced down at my white-knuckled grip on the two armrests of my seat. Maybe it was too late. My level of fear was already at its max.

Are you kidding me, God? Was all I could think. *I've traveled halfway around the world to find meaning in my life, and I finally found it. Now this? I'm going to crash and burn on this plane before I get to use any of my newfound knowledge. Are you kidding me?*

Then I started to calm myself down. I decided to control my thoughts instead of letting my thoughts control me. Well, at least I had found the meaning I was searching for before I bit the dust. I was grateful for that. Besides, if I was going to meet my maker, I was ready. I decided I had lived a great but short life. It was ironic the plane was ascending and diving like a roller coaster. It was just one more metaphor of my life . . . just a series of ups and downs. I closed my eyes in another attempt to calm myself and then reached for Greg's hand.

My thoughts were interrupted by the shouts of a large elderly gentleman who was sitting across the aisle, five rows in front of us. He was obviously scared out of his mind and was calling for a stewardess. One brave flight attendant ventured down the aisle holding on to the seatbacks in order to maintain her balance. When she reached the gentleman, she knelt down beside him to not only be at his eye level, but also because she could no longer stand up as the plane careened through the air. I had no idea what they said to each other. I assumed he was sharing his fears, and she was trying to console him. One thing that was crystal clear was the intensity of the grip he had on her shoulder. As she stood to return to her seat, he desperately tried to pull her back, but she successfully avoided his grasp.

The flight attendant was gone only a matter of minutes when the pilot announced that we had arrived at the Denver International Airport, but due to the severe weather, we wouldn't be able to land. Instead, we were in a "holding pattern" flying over the airport for an indefinite amount of time. Instantly, the older gentleman began screaming for the stewardess again. She had no choice but to return to his seat to console him. His continual shouting was heightening the fear of the rest of the passengers.

As this scenario played out in front of me, I was reminded of the last few days I spent with my father before he passed away. When Dad was in his fifties he had a cancerous lung removed, so he had spent a large portion of his adult life dealing with breathing

225

problems. As he aged, living with one lung became more difficult and being diagnosed with heart failure added to his health problems. Dad had checked himself into the local nursing home, which was owned by my sister, Barb, and her husband. Even though he received excellent care, his condition worsened until finally Barb called to tell me it was time to come home and say good-bye to our father. School was in session, but I managed to obtain a substitute teacher for a week so I could fly back to Iowa.

While I was home visiting, some nights I spent at Barb's house, which was across the street from the care facility. Some nights I spent at Dad's empty house, but most of the nights I spent sleeping in the recliner in the corner of Dad's private room. Often he would awake in the middle of the night, gasping for breath, and calling for help. I would rush to the side of his bed, and he would clutch my shirt drawing me close to his terror stricken eyes.

"I'm dying! I can't breathe!" he would gasp.

I would try my best to calm him, telling him he was going to be all right, and encouraging him to calm down, which would help his breathing. He, in turn, would insist that I call the local priest. Our parish priest had visited Dad on a daily basis, bringing Holy Communion, praying, and administering the last rites several times. Although Dad was always calmed by the presence of the priest, there was no way I was going to call the holy man in the middle of the night, each and every night.

Eventually, the fact that Dad was afraid of dying made it to the nursing staff and finally to his doctor. Hoping to alleviate his fear, the doctor stopped in at Dad's room one afternoon to explain in detail what it was going to be like when he died. Basically, the physician told Dad he was going to go to sleep and not wake up. Dad insisted he was going to choke or suffocate, but the doctor assured him that he would prescribe a medication to help with his breathing difficulties.

I thought the conversation with the doctor had helped my father, until that evening when he woke up in the middle of the night gasping for breath and pleading for me to call the priest. When I finally calmed him down, I grabbed him by the shoulders to focus his attention.

"Dad, look at me," I commanded. "Why are you so afraid of dying? Tell me now."

"I don't know what it will be like," he admitted. "I know the doctor told me what dying would be like, but I don't know what it will be like after I am dead."

Silence.

I couldn't believe what I was hearing. This was a man of faith. A man who had a holy card and a set of rosary beads tucked in the pocket of his suit coat jacket every Sunday at church. This was a man who said meal prayers, went to every funeral of his friends and family members, and never missed mass on Sundays or holy days. Was that all just superficial? Was that all just a ritual? Did any of that have meaning for him? Did he really have a relationship with God or was he just going through the motions? It was time to find out.

"Dad, don't you believe you are going to heaven? Don't you believe you've led a good life?" I asked him. "Don't you believe in God?"

"I don't know any more," he admitted.

"What do you believe?" I pushed.

Silence.

"Here's what I believe," I started. "I think the doctor is right in that you are going to go to sleep, but I disagree that you won't wake up. I know you will wake up, but you will wake up in the presence of God. Isn't that our ultimate goal? To make it to heaven. You are a good person, Dad. You've led a good life. You've been a good and faithful servant. You are going to heaven. There's no doubt about that in my mind."

Silence.

He rolled over on his side with his back toward me, and I knew our conversation was over. I never did know if Dad ever came to grips with death. I could only stay one more day after that fateful night then I had to return home to my family and my job. Dad and I said our good-byes knowing it would be the last time we would see each other on this planet, but I knew I would see him again in heaven. I could only hope he believed that, too.

The frightened man on our plane was desperately clinging to the flight attendant just as Dad had hung on to the priest. I think in times of fear it is a common reaction for human beings to hold onto something or someone. People or things are tangible representations of the intangible concept of hope. Dad felt the priest could give him hope that he wouldn't die, or if he did die, the priest would be the bridge from this life to the next. The man on the plane must have felt the stewardess was his hope. He wanted her to tell him everything was going to be all right. He wanted to hear that the storm was going to pass, and the plane was going to land safely. In each case, both men needed to let go of the person who symbolized hope to them. They needed to put their hope in God, but that's a difficult thing to do. You can grasp the flight attendant's shoulder when she is kneeling next to you. You can see the priest standing next to your hospital bed, but you can't see or touch God. That's where faith comes into play. You have to believe God is right there beside you even though you can 't see or touch Him. That is what faith is all about . . . believing and trusting in God. It's a hard lesson to learn that you have to let go of something to reach for something better.

It seemed as though we had been circling the airport for an extended period of time, all the while tossing and churning in the air. The calm voice of the pilot filled the cabin once again. Of course, we were all hoping he was going to tell us we would be landing soon, but that was not the case. In a tranquil voice, he explained that we were running out of fuel. If we did not receive clearance to land within the next ten to fifteen minutes, we would be heading south to land at the airport in Colorado Springs.

Are you kidding me, Lord? Is this some kind of test? Are you trying to get my attention? I know there are times when You are trying to reveal something to me, and I'm just not paying attention, but I'm paying attention now! I've learned a lesson on this trip. It's the interaction between people and the interaction of people with God that gives life meaning. I intend to put this new knowledge into action as soon as this plane lands. I am willing to let go of whatever you want me to let go of and put my faith, trust, and hope in You.

Bam! As soon as the pilot finished the announcement, the elderly gentleman began bellowing for the flight attendant again. In my opinion, that guy needed to "chill lax. He needed to put his trust and faith in God and just let go.

Chapter 27
The Art of Letting Go

Eventually, we were able to land at the Denver airport. The older gentleman was one of the first people to be able to leave the plane from the economy section.

We were thankful to return to our home, to see it still standing in the majestic pines of the Black Forest. By July 1st, the Waldo Canyon Fire was fifty-five percent contained, and thirty-five thousand people were able to return to their homes. The fire wouldn't be one hundred percent contained until July 10th. In the end, two people lost their lives. Three hundred forty-six homes were destroyed, and over eighteen thousand acres were burned. Mudslides and flooding occurred months and even years later as a direct result of the fire destroying much of the natural vegetation. So much for man and nature coexisting in harmony.

When August arrived, I was eager to implement my new understandings I had learned in France into the fabric of my life. I was eager to treat my students as masterpieces, but before I could do that, there were many changes to adjust to. For one thing, I wasn't waiting for the results of a needle biopsy like last August. Landon started sixth grade, his last year in the elementary school at which I taught. Sierra had started her senior year of high school, and Greg had begun one more year as a middle school assistant principal. I had welcomed a fresh group of eager third graders into my classroom. Once the school year began for each of us, we settled into a routine. Our lives were even-keeled, and downright normal, but I could feel in my heart a storm was brewing on the horizon.

I have often felt that living life is much like climbing a ladder in that you must let go of the ladder rung you are on before you can reach for the next one. But there is something about the comfort, safety, and familiarity of the rung you are on that makes you cling to it even though you know the next step up is going to be even better. During the tumultuous plane ride that summer, I had made a promise to God that I would be willing to let go of whatever He wanted me to let go of, in order to reach for a deeper, lasting relationship with Him.

I realized it was time for me to fulfill my promise, but God was asking me to let go of something I loved, something that over the years had come to define me, something that gave me a purpose and a reason for living. What was that something? My career. It was heartbreaking for me to let go, but I trusted God. I trusted that God was willing to pry my hand off that rung of life's ladder one finger at a time. Through His loving and patient lessons, He taught me the art of letting go.

I think most people who have been on a cancer journey will tell you it is a process, which changes you forever. Obviously, my cancer experience changed me physically, but I didn't realize how much my cancer journey and our trip to France had changed me emotionally and spiritually until I started the new school year.

Because they were almost taken from me, I had developed a deeper appreciation for life and a new concept regarding time. Now, I viewed both time and life as priceless, precious treasures, and I guarded their use with every ounce of my being. Events and activities I once felt were important, now seemed to be overrated.

Through our French excursion, I had come to the understanding that people are masterpieces, which are unique, precious, and valuable. Yet I found myself caught in the educational system, which wanted to turn the students and me into robots. I was expected to churn out students who were all the same, as if they were products on a factory assembly line. I didn't feel it was my job as a teacher to pour knowledge into human beings in order to insure continuity. I had always believed it was my calling to be a guide who draws out the unique gifts and talents of each individual and to help people to develop to their highest levels of potential. This process is unique, and as individual as each person. There is nothing "cookie cutter" about it. I believed my students were masterpieces; pieces of work of outstanding artistry, skill, and workmanship, not identical, uniform human beings represented by numbers, letters, graphs, and charts.

Every two to three years, the elementary school teachers in the district where I worked were faced with a new report card, which no one understood. Teachers, students, and parents would grapple with each new round of numbers, letters, and symbols in an attempt to make sense of each student's progress. The process involved with each new report card took an exorbitant amount of time. This was time, which could have been spent planning lessons, teaching, learning, or living. Most people forget that time is finite. There is only a certain amount of time. Twenty-four hours in a day to be exact. You can't make more time, so if you decide to spend time on an activity, then you must take time away from something else.

You don't have to be diagnosed with cancer to understand the importance of time. In fact, the cold, hard reality is that we all have a terminal illness. It's called life. None of us are going to live forever. The sooner you come to grips with this concept, the better your life is going to become. To use time wisely was the lesson I had learned.

The report cards were just the tip of the iceberg when it came to work related activities I believed were a total waste of time and a waste of my life. After many years in the field of education, I had the wisdom to know when something was a fad and wouldn't last. A new outdoor curriculum was headed our way, and it had fad written all over it. Backward lesson planning was another fad being forced on the educators in the district. Just the very use of the word "backward" should have indicated its level of usefulness and intelligence. Finally, there was the electronic portfolio teachers were supposed to create in order to prove their value and worth. The hours, days, weeks, and months this electronic debacle sucked up was mind-boggling. From my viewpoint, if you wanted to know the value and worth of an educator, you simply sat in a classroom and watched him or her teach.

These situations were like the screeching of fingernails on a chalkboard to me. Perhaps that was what God had intended in order to get my full attention because He was about to impart His wisdom to me through a series of experiences and lessons. With each lesson, God would pry one of my fingers from the rung of life's ladder, and I would learn the art of letting go. I had just learned lesson one; let go of things that are a waste of time, and with that realization, I released my thumb from the death grip it had on my current situation.

I have always believed that God doesn't make junk. His creations are glorious, wonderful, exciting, unique, and beautiful because they come from Him. This is especially true of human beings because we are created in His likeness. That is how I felt about each student who was ever in my class. I could see through the behavior or academic challenges to see the image of God, to see the gifts, talents, and potential God had given each individual. I saw every child as unique, special, and different. Through the school district's rules and policies, it was clear what I believed in wasn't valued or even honored. The focus on standardized test scores, lackluster curriculums, and statistics was turning students and teachers into numbers rather than cultivating their humanness.

After a year on our cancer journey, the staff and students at our school had changed. We had looked long and hard at our lives, our mortality, our relationships, and our purposes. It was difficult for me to go from that type of thinking to multiple-choice test questions on the state's standardized test.

The school district was asking me to hook kids up to computers, to pour what knowledge they deemed essential into the students when I believed I should have been drawing out and utilizing the gifts and talents within them. The school district was charging me with the task of making each child the same, as if I were a factory worker on an assembly line creating a product. In my heart, I knew God was charging me with the task of nurturing each child in order to release, utilize, and cultivate their gifts with the ultimate goal being for each student to become the best human being, the best likeness of God, that he or she could become. This was quite a dichotomy, which was not only tearing at my heart but at my very soul. This thinking of polar opposites led me to lesson two; let go of what you don't believe in. Upon this discovery, my index finger had released its grasp from the ladder rung.

At this time, the school board in the district where I was employed had been taken over by a group of people calling themselves the reformers. The reformers were actually a nation-wide group who were attempting to gain control of school districts across the country. One distinct goal of this group was to rid school districts of veteran teachers in order to not only silence their voices and squelch their wisdom, but also to replace them with younger, inexperienced teachers who they could hire at a much lower cost, and who they could control.

As a veteran teacher, I felt as if I had an enormous target painted on my chest. Ironically, it was the chest I had just spent a year trying to save. It was a chest that had become a symbol of my battle for life and my battle to bring new meaning to my existence. It was also the chest that contained my heart, a heart that knew right from wrong. I knew in my heart that what the reformers were doing was wrong. It was wrong for everyone involved . . . staff members, students, parents, families, and community members. It was wrong to treat children as numbers, products, and statistics. It was wrong to single out a group of people because of their ages and experiences and to treat them with such disrespect. The bullseye imprinted on each veteran teacher's chest were symbols that we were fair game.

With this constant barrage of negativity directed at me, I began to doubt myself. I no longer believed in myself, and that was dangerous because if I didn't believe in myself, how could I teach my students to believe in themselves. It was through this train of thought that I learned the third lesson God was trying to teach me; let go of people and situations that continually hurt you and others. With that lesson, God pried my middle finger off the ladder rung I was so desperately clinging to.

It doesn't take a math wizard to realize I was now hanging on to my career with two fingers, but those two fingers had an iron grip. This was a pivotal point. Should I keep hanging on, or let go? I didn't know what to do so I did what I always do in times of indecision, or should I say times of decision? I asked God for help.

God's answer to my request for help came in an unexpected form, my friend Chris. Chris is not only my friend but also my financial advisor. Each fall,

237

he showed up at our home on a Saturday for an annual review of our finances.

Chris' family, like ours, had recently been on a cancer journey. His father and father-in-law had simultaneously been diagnosed with prostate cancer. His father survived. His father-in-law did not. I admired Chris for how he dealt with the situation. He threw himself into raising money to further the awareness, treatment and research for a cure for this type of cancer. His tireless efforts did not go unnoticed. I knew by helping others, he was trying to deal with his loss in the most constructive way he knew possible. I knew because I had been in his situation myself.

We sat at the dining room table, as we always did for these meetings. As usual, I brought him a glass of ice water and a plate of his favorite chocolate chip cookies fresh from the oven. All things considered, it seemed like one of our routine meetings until Chris opened his mouth and spoke.

He looked me right in the eyes and said, "I think you should retire."

Suddenly, all of the air was sucked out of my lungs. I loved my career. I had been a teacher since high school, tutoring elementary students and helping my mom with religious education classes. Granted, I did complain periodically about the red tape and politics involved with education, but once the classroom door closed, I was in my element. I built real relationships with the students. I loved each and every student as if they were my own children. Learning was fun, and life was cherished in our classroom, and we laughed. We laughed a lot. Teaching gave my life purpose and meaning. It had become an essential part of my identity. How could I give all of that up?

"I've given this a lot of thought," Chris continued. "I have a plan I would like to share with you."

I finally exhaled and tried to calm myself so I could concentrate on what Chris was saying.

"I want you to do the things you've always dreamed of doing; travel, be with your family, hang out with your friends, pursue a hobby. Whatever it is you want to do, I want you to do it, and do it now . . . before it is too late," he said as he broke eye contact with me looking down at the tabletop.

I knew where this was coming from. Chris' father and father-in-law were about my age. They were men who were thinking their golden years were just ahead of them only to have that vision crushed by a cancer diagnosis and for one of them to have his life taken from him. Chris knew about my cancer diagnosis, and now he was putting all the pieces from my experience and his together to benefit me.

Chris had a dual insight into my world. He understood my cancer journey and how it had changed my perspective on . . . everything. Chris also had insight into my work world because the majority of his clients and his wife were employed by the same school district.

"I know what is going on in the school district, and I don't anticipate it getting any better," he added. "You are within the retirement range, and I can make it happen for you so you won't have to worry about money. Will you let me do that for you?"

I couldn't breathe, but this time it wasn't due to shock. It was because at that moment in time I realized the true depth of Chris' friendship, and I was trying desperately not to cry.

Chris opened his portfolio, spilling several pieces of paper onto the table. As he shared his notes, graphs, and diagrams, I knew he wasn't only sharing documents, but also his hopes and dreams for me. As I watched him explain the diversification of my assets, I gazed at the intense look on his face. I smiled because I knew I was looking at a true and trusted friend.

Lesson four had been learned from the heart and gestures of a real friend; in order for you to feel comfortable letting go, you have to have something new to reach towards. For me, that something new was retirement. My ring finger let go of that ladder rung. Now I was holding on by just my pinkie.

Small, often forgotten and certainly underestimated, that is what the pinkie finger is all about. Certainly that was true in this case because for me the pinkie finger was symbolic of faith. Faith is often forgotten and certainly underestimated; yet it holds the power and keys to many of life's challenges and situations.

In order to finally let go of the ladder rung I was on and to reach for the next rung, I needed to have faith that God would not let me fall. It was a choice between fear, which pierced my heart driving me into a state of numbness and indecision, or faith, which had the power to enlighten my path and enrich my life. It seemed like a "no brainer" to me, so I let go.

My fifth and final lesson had been learned; have faith in God. When my pinkie finger let go, I was finally able to reach for the next rung on life's ladder. From my new, higher vantage point, I was able to view more of what God had planned for me.

Chapter 28
When I Was a Girl, I Dreamed

Apparently I wasn't the only person who had learned the art of letting go. The mass exodus of educators from the district was astounding. Hundreds of teachers retired early or took new jobs in other school districts. In our tiny school of approximately three hundred students, eight teachers, including me, retired that year.

As I glanced around my empty classroom, tears started to form in my eyes, but no one was around to witness my sorrow. I had come to school on a Saturday to clean out my classroom with a promise I would turn my key in on Monday, the first day of summer break. It had taken the entire day to pack my room. It's amazing what teachers purchase for their classrooms out of their own pockets. Not only were there regular school supplies including crayons, pencils, paper, and notebooks, but bookshelves, chairs, stools, games, math materials, equipment for science experiments, books, books, and more books. For the entire week, I had been taking home a carload of boxes each day, but today was my last load.

I had left the wall behind the table we used for reading groups as the last thing to dismantle. It was symbolic for me. Hanging on that wall was my teaching certificate along with my diplomas representing many of the degrees and honors I had earned. I had encouraged other teachers to have similar walls in their classrooms with the hope that this physical representation of our education levels and experiences would one day earn us the same respect as doctors, lawyers, engineers, and business people. *Who was I kidding? That was never going to happen, at least not in my lifetime.*

I removed my framed teaching certificate from the wall, wrapped it in newspaper, and placed it in the nearest box. A few tears dripped onto the paper and the flaps of the box. At this point, I didn't care. I reached up to remove the next framed document. Only it wasn't a document. It was a print I had purchased from an artist/writer, Mark Ludy, who periodically visited our school to inspire our staff and students with his assemblies. I had always found Mark to be such a fascinating, creative, and fun-loving person, so after his assemblies, I would invite him to our classroom so the kids could just "love on him" for a while. The kids and I would present him with thank you notes, letters, and cards exalting his skills as a writer and artist. On one of his trips to our school, I purchased a print from him, which was in a book he had illustrated titled <u>When I Was Girl . . . I Dreamed</u>. I had promptly framed the print and added it to my "wall of pride" as a reminder of what I had dreamed of as a girl.

I glanced down at the print I held in my hands. I was shocked! I grabbed the nearest chair and sat down. I had expected to see the illustration from the fourth page of the book, which was a drawing of a teacher in her classroom. For many years I had thought I had purchased that print, but what I saw before me was Mark's illustration found later in the book. It was a writer sitting at a table in her home surrounded by a computer, stacks of books, and piles of crumpled papers. The best part of the illustration was the enormous smile on the woman's face as she pounded out a fantastic piece of writing on the keyboard in front of her.

"Thank you, God," I murmured as I drew the framed piece of artwork close to my chest. I felt a warmth radiate from the drawing into my entire body. I knew what I was going to do. I knew what I was going to be or perhaps it was what I had always been . . . a writer.

When I was a girl, I loved writing. I wrote poems and turned them into greeting cards. I had a journal and wrote stories, but my favorite thing to do was to write plays. Even as a teacher, I had written plays for the students to perform at assemblies. To me, the fact that letters on a page form words, which have meaning and create images in our imaginations and emotions in our souls, is nothing short of magic. That is the beauty of writing.

I placed the framed print in a nearby box and quickly retrieved the rest of the framed documents from the wall. There was a new spring in my step as I carried that last box to my car and popped it into the backseat. The outside door to my classroom had locked behind me one last time, but I felt at peace because another door had been opened. I was reminded that so often in my life I had asked God for help and guidance, and He had never failed to answer my prayers. This case was no different. The answer to my prayer as to what to do next had been hanging on the wall of my classroom for many years. All I had to do was to take the time to look at it.

Chapter 29
Turn the Page

I feel blessed that for many years I was able to teach people of all ages how to read. One key comprehension strategy I instilled in my students was knowing when to turn the page. This may sound so simple that it is on the edge of being ridiculous. Think about this for a moment. How many times have you made it to the bottom of a page only to realize you have no idea or understanding about what you just read? Somehow your mind wanders, or you begin to daydream. Before you know it, you are at the bottom of the page without a clue as to what you just read. Should you turn the page? Of course not. If you don't stop to reread the page, you won't understand the information on the pages that follow.

Life has often been compared to a book. Each stage such as childhood, teenage years, adulthood, parenthood, and retirement are all chapters. But we must not forget that within these chapters are pages to be turned in order to move forward. The key to life is knowing when to turn the page, when to reread, and when to stop to savor what you just experienced. As I entered into the retirement chapter of my life, I felt like I was flipping through the pages at a fairly rapid pace.

Sierra and I had decided to combine her graduation with my retirement. It seemed appropriate. She was graduating from high school, and I was graduating from . . . third grade. We planned a wonderful party for our family members and our friends. It was an afternoon filled with delicious food, time for reminiscing and discussions of future plans, and time for laughter. The only disappointing aspect of our dual graduation party was that it occurred at the same time as the Relay for Life back in Iowa. It was one more year that Barb and I were unable to complete our survivor lap. As always, she understood about the situation. When all of the graduation and retirement festivities were completed, it was time to turn the page.

With Sierra heading off to college in the fall, and Landon attending the middle school where Greg worked, we decided to sell our home in order to relocate closer to Greg and Landon's school. As soon as this decision was made, home improvement became my new full time job. We made a list of tasks that needed to be completed before we could put our house on the market. Since Greg worked during the summers, the list became my responsibility. I must have done a bang up job because once we put our home on the market; it sold in less than twenty-four hours. Turn the page.

Selling our home so quickly was totally unexpected. We had not even looked for a new place to live. Once again, we put our faith in God to provide for us. After one day of searching, we found the perfect home. In a blink of an eye, my new job title became Packing/Moving Guru.

I quickly learned the amount of stuff a family of four can accumulate over twenty years is mindboggling. I decided to take our moving situation as an opportunity to purge, not just a little, but major purging. Soon I was on a first name basis with the attendant at the local Goodwill Donation Center. Then I reached professional status at selling items online, and I developed the ability to make split second decisions regarding whether an item was useful or just plain trash.

Once the weeks of purging were complete, the packing stage began. From sunrise to sunset, I expertly packed and labeled boxes. When Greg and Landon arrived home from school each night, they would load Greg's truck with the boxes I had packed that day. After school, they would transport and unload the cargo into a storage unit near our new home. Then the entire cycle would start all over again. This went on for several weeks until I was totally exhausted. Fortunately, the closings for both homes occurred on the same day only a few hours apart. By the end of October we were completely moved into our new home. Turn the page.

Finally, I had time to write. For lack of a better term, the fact I could write every day was absolutely delicious. I especially treasured the cold winter days when I could curl up with a quilt, a mug of hot tea, a spiral notebook, and a pen. I was finally able to delve into the very depths of my imagination. What I found there was shocking, even to me. Hidden in my creative self was a science fiction story. This was shocking because I rarely read science fiction, let alone wrote it.

The book I wrote was about a young doctor who spends ten years researching ways to regenerate cells in an effort to heal his damaged spinal cord, which has left him in a wheelchair. Through his research, the doctor discovers a way to not only improve people's health issues, but also a way to control their memories and lives. Throughout the book the doctor battles himself in an effort to decide whether he is truly helping people or possibly taking on the role of God, deciding who lives and who dies. With such deep subject matter, by the time I finished writing at the end of each day, I was mentally and emotionally drained, but I was persistent and by the end of December the book was finished. Turn the page.

I had promised myself to celebrate each birthday I was given with zest and passion. Since my birthday is during the last week of January, and my husband's birthday is the first week in February, we always celebrated our birthdays together. Often we took advantage of the fact that the Super Bowl took place about this time by hosting a birthday/Super Bowl party. That is exactly what we had planned for this year, but without my knowledge, Greg had invited a few surprise guests.

On my actual birthday, Greg called from work to tell me he had to supervise an after-school sporting event so he would be home late.

"Don't eat because I'm going to take you out for dinner for your birthday," he told me. "It's just going to be a little later than we thought."

No problem. I thought. The time didn't matter. I just didn't want to cook on my birthday.

About 8 p.m. there was a knock on the door that led to the garage. No one ever knocked on that door. Usually it was the front door. I was almost afraid to open it, but I was glad I did. There standing before me were my three sisters. I screamed in delight, jumping up and down in some sort of strange display of raw emotion. My sisters all lived in Iowa and rarely left the state. If they did, it was in a car and certainly not on an airplane.

"I can't believe it!" I screamed repeatedly as I embraced each sister until her eyes bulged out of her head. Once Greg, the sisters and their luggage were all safely inside, the story of the birthday surprise quickly unfolded. Greg and my sisters had been plotting and planning this trip for several months. Greg hadn't been at school that evening. He had driven to Denver to pick up my sisters at the airport. I could tell by the smug look on all four of their faces, they thought they were exceedingly sly and clever.

When my mom was alive, whenever she spoke about Greg, she would always say, "That Greg, he is such a prince." He was a prince. In fact, he was my knight in shining armor. He patiently loaded the four giggling sisters and Landon into his truck and proceeded to drive us to the Italian restaurant we had originally planned to dine at. I had offered to sit in the backseat, but the sisters wanted no part of that deal. They wanted Landon to join them so they could interrogate their beloved nephew.

"How is school going?"

"What classes are you taking?"

"Is it weird to have your dad as your assistant principal?"

"Do you have a girlfriend?"

"When are you coming to Iowa to visit us?"

Landon is such a shy person. I wasn't sure how he would fare when up against the sisters. But when I peered in the rearview mirror, I could tell by his expression that he loved all of the attention.

The six of us squeezed into a large booth at the restaurant. As I looked across the table, I still couldn't believe my three sisters were here, alive and in the flesh. Clearly, they intended to give their baby sister a birthday to remember. I truly was the baby of the group.

Barb, who was sixteen years older than me, had always been like my second mother. After our mother passed away, Barb became the matriarch of our family.

Jan was two years younger than Barb. She often compared herself to our oldest sister and struggled to see her unique talents and gifts. She had our dad's wonderful sense of humor and our mom's unbridled laugh.

Mary was eight years my senior. We shared a room growing up, but I use the word share loosely because she was clearly the one in charge. I knew in my heart she had been the one to think of the birthday surprise, and she was the one who probably had arranged all of the details to make the trip a reality.

Over appetizers and dinner, the three sisters shared their airport escapades. As I had thought, Mary was the ringleader of the group. We all knew Barb had a deep, dark fear of escalators, which forced Mary to search out stairs and elevators as a way of getting to and from the various levels of the airports. Jan had limited flying experience so when asked to go through the metal detector, she walked through it as if it were a doorway. The sisters laughed as they retold the story.

"The TSA workers had to walk Jan through step by step," Mary explained. "She didn't know you had to stop, raise your arms, and wait for the scanners to move around you."

"How was I supposed to know?" Jan questioned.

"Didn't you watch the people in front of you?" I asked.

"I was too busy removing my shoes and other articles of clothing. I was lucky to still be wearing my underwear by the time they told me to walk through that contraption," Jan laughed.

Of course we ended the meal with a rousing rendition of the happy birthday song and three desserts we passed around the table so we could all sample a little of each delicious treat. The sisters deviously tricked the waiter into giving them the bill. Visions of The Three Stooges stirred in my head as I watched them banter about how to split the check between the three of them.

When we were back in the truck, Landon conveniently checked out and took a short nap so the sisters directed their questions at me.

"How do you like retirement?"

"Have you met many of your neighbors?"

"What have you been doing with yourself?"

"When are you coming back to Iowa to visit?"

Once we reached our house Greg, Landon, and Barb headed off to bed, but Mary, Jan, and I decided to stay up to play card games. Since the bedroom Barb was sleeping in was next to the dining room where we were playing cards, we kept our laughter to a dull roar. It wasn't long before we could hear Barb's trademark snoring.

"She really needs to get that snoring problem checked out," Jan said nodding her head in the direction of Barb's bedroom.

"How is she doing?" I asked as I threw a card into the discard pile.

Barb's cancer was back. Like me, she had been blindsided. She thought she was in the ring with melanoma. She had her boxing gloves on and had taken a defensive stance with hands up to protect her face, and arms tucked in to her sides to protect her abdomen. She was facing her opponent head on ready for battle when colon cancer snuck up and gave her a left hook to the gut.

"She seems to be doing okay," Mary explained as she picked up the card I had just discarded. "It's hard to tell with her. We did have to arrange this trip around her chemotherapy treatments. She just finished a round so she is on a break right now."

"Her hair is getting thinner, but other than that she looks really good," I added.

"You know she named her colostomy bag Carl, right?" Jan asked me as she fanned the cards in her hand.

Barb's many surgeries had included having a large section of her colon removed and a colostomy bag attached to the outside of her abdomen to do the job of her damaged colon. The bag was covered by her clothing and wasn't noticeable.

"Yeah, we talk on the phone," I explained. "She told me Carl doesn't talk much and basically just hangs around."

"That's nothing," Jan added. "Usually she tells everyone that Carl is an asshole."

We all laughed. That was so like Barb to find humor in a normally dismal situation.

"She bonded with one of the flight attendants on the way here. The lady had a relative who had recently been diagnosed with cancer, and Barb was giving her a run down of what to expect, and what to do to help," Mary explained. "She does that wherever she goes, and I admire her for that."

"Hey, she did it for me," I added. "I am glad you all came to celebrate my birthday. But I'm especially glad you brought Barb so I could actually see how she is doing. When I talk to her on the phone, she always paints a picture that everything is sunshine and rainbows. There is nothing about having cancer that is sunshine and rainbows."

"She just needs to deal with it in her own way. If that is with humor and positive thinking, then so be it," Jan said adding a card to her hand.

"You're right. I know from experience that is totally true," I added. "I just worry about her, and being so far away makes my mind think of the worst possible scenarios."

"We promise to keep you updated on her condition. Right, Jan?" Mary offered.

"We will," Jan agreed. "Let's call it a night and go to bed, girls."

We spent the next several days exploring several tourist sites in the Colorado Springs area, eating delicious food, playing cards into the late night hours, and laughing.

One afternoon Mary suggested a short walk in the neighborhood to look at the new homes that were under construction, and to work off some of the calories we had ingested earlier in the day. Midway through the hike, a light snow began to fall. Always the instigator, Mary suggested we make snow angels. Jan, Mary, and I flopped to the ground on the nearest empty lot and began swishing our arms and legs across the surface of the snow.

"Come on, Barb. Join us!" I called.

"I'd love to, but I think once I get down on the ground I won't be able to get back up," she replied.

We respected her decision and proudly proclaimed her to be the Official Snow Angel Supervisor. When the snow angels were completed, Mary and I were able to maneuver ourselves back to an upright position. It was a different story for Jan mainly because she was laughing uncontrollably. Mary and I each grabbed one of her hands, gave a tug, and she popped back into a vertical stance. Now we were all laughing. My sisters and I hadn't grown up together. When I was born, Barb and Jan were teenagers, and Mary was in elementary school. When I was in elementary school, they were all married ladies. For a few fleeting moments that afternoon, as we romped and played in the snow, we were ageless, living a childhood we had never experienced together. Just as the intricate snowflakes landed briefly on our jackets then melted quickly, so did our worries. We were four adult women who over several decades had dealt with the stress of our jobs, the responsibility of raising children, the insurmountable challenge of being a woman in a man's world, and the constant concern over health issues including dealing with cancer. All those cares and concerns melted away as we caught snowflakes on our tongues, threw handfuls of snow at each other, made snow angels, and giggled uncontrollably. Time stood still as we shared a brief moment of childhood together. It was a moment I didn't want to end, a page I didn't want to turn. Not because I didn't understand the meaning of the passage, but because it was my favorite part of the book. I wanted to savor it, reading it over and over until it was imprinted in my mind . . . forever.

Sisters

Chapter 30
The Gift of Love

Our carefree attitudes spilled over to the Super Bowl/birthday party. It was fun to introduce my sisters to my friends. The sisters had all inherited our parents' outgoing personalities. Mary was an avid football fan and enjoyed watching the game and shouting at the television with the rest of us. Jan and Barb were content visiting with the guests, enjoying the snacks, and watching "The Puppy Bowl" which was playing on the television in the master bedroom.

As the old saying goes, "Every good thing must come to an end," and the sisters had to pack up their bags and return to their lives in Iowa. Our good-bye wasn't difficult because I knew I would be seeing them in less than two weeks.

When Chris, our financial advisor, told me he wanted me to do all the things I wanted to do, I actually sat down and made a list of those activities. One of the top ten on the list was to help my niece Allison, a flower shop owner, make her Valentine's Day deliveries. Valentine's Day was the busiest day of the year for the flower shop. For years, my sisters had helped our niece with the deliveries. Each year they would share with me stories of their adventures and the fun of being together on the holiday dedicated to love. I loved to hear about their escapades, but I was also disheartened because I could never participate when I was working, but that was no longer the case. Several months in advance, I had purchased an airline ticket to go back to Iowa for Valentine's Day.

Our parents had passed away several years ago and their home had been sold, so when I returned to our hometown, I stayed with Barb. She was divorced. Her son was grown and gone, so she lived alone in a gigantic house on the west side of town. When I was in elementary school, I had what I considered to be my own room at Barb's home. She often referred to it as the guest room, but I knew in my heart it had been created with one specific guest in mind . . . me. The room had a twin bed with a flowery bedspread and matching curtains. It was filled with toys, dolls, and stuffed animals, which normally are not guest bedroom items.

On Valentine's Day, it was still dark when Barb and I rolled out of bed and made the five-minute drive to the flower shop. After many years, Allison and my sisters had the art of spreading Valentine's Day love down to a science. Jan was Allison's wingman or wingwoman in this case, staying at the flower shop to help make the arrangements, which would be ordered that day. The rest of the assistants delivered all the love in the form of flowers, balloons, candy, cards, and stuffed animals. The "love team" had learned over the years not to send people out alone to make the deliveries. Uncertain Midwest weather and uncertain reactions from a few of the love recipients had dictated that the deliveries be made by teams of two people also known as cupids. Mary and I had decided to be one delivery team, while Barb was teamed up with a friend of our niece.

When Barb and I arrived at the flower shop, Mary already had her car loaded for the first delivery so I quickly joined her. As I opened the car door to hop into the passenger seat, I glanced at the backseat. Love always seems to be a concept or idea to me, not something tangible. But if you could see love, it was definitely what I saw in the back of my sister's car. It was filled with boxes of stuffed animals. Each one had a Valentine's Day helium balloon attached, along with a small card, and a candy bar.

"Where are we going?" I questioned Mary as I surveyed the contents of her car.

"To the daycare center," she informed me. *Ah, the stuffed animals, I should have guessed.* "Trust me. This is going to be fun! You are going to love it!" she added. I loved it already, and we hadn't even reached our destination.

Mary owned the Dairy Queen in town. She operated it during the summer months, and the rest of the year she worked part time at the daycare center so she knew all the children at the facility. When we walked into the center, the children crowded around Mary calling her name. Obviously they thought she was working that day.

"We've brought you Valentine's Day gifts!" she announced. "When we call your name, come and get your gift." The kids were intelligent enough to know they needed to be quiet in order to hear their names being called, and Mary's take charge demeanor also helped to subdue the crowd of excited preschoolers.

Mary positioned herself at one end of the room while I was at the other side. As soon as I called a name, a child would appear before me screaming with delight. Knowing the children couldn't read the attached cards, I would tell them who the gift was from, and usually it was from their parents or grandparents.

"Thank you, thank you, thank you," each child exclaimed as he or she hugged my legs simply because that was as far as they could reach. I could definitely feel the love. The "leg hugs," the accolades, and the endearing sweet smiles were my Valentine's Day gifts. What a way to start the day. I couldn't imagine that it could get any better, but it did.

We headed back to the flower shop to reload the car for our next delivery. This time the back seat became a sea of red and white roses and carnations. The aroma was nothing short of heavenly. Once again the car was bursting with physical symbols of love.

"Where are we headed to this time?" I asked Mary as I took my designated place in the shotgun position in the front seat.

"The nursing home," she answered with a huge smile on her face.

"Sweet!" I responded as I smiled back at her. Barb and her husband had owned the local nursing home for several years before selling it in order to enter other business opportunities. Our family had always spent a lot of time at the local care center. We loved the facility and what it stood for. We loved the staff and residents. Over the years, many of the residents had become like family members.

Even though we hadn't purchased any of the flower arrangements for the residents, we were the lucky recipients of many hugs from the seniors who lived at the care center. Even the residents who didn't receive flowers were overjoyed by our presence and by the flowers, which soon adorned the front desk, the rooms, and the tables in the dining area.

Our next two or three carloads of love were delivered to schools in the surrounding small towns. The variety of the symbols of love for these deliveries was amazing. There were flower arrangements, stuffed animals, helium balloons, bouquets of candy bars, and sometimes it was a single carnation or rose wrapped in beautiful cellophane and tied with pink or red ribbon.

No matter where we went, we were greeted with the same warm reception; with hugs, smiles, and an unending supply of "thank yous." Part of the strategic plan was to deliver to personal residences at the end of the day when most people were home from work. We began this stage of the process by making deliveries to the rural areas so that we wouldn't be out on the country roads in the dark. We completed the day with deliveries to homes within the city limits.

It was late in the evening when our mission to spread love to people of all ages in a multitude of counties in rural Iowa ended. Even though we had volunteered our services as cupids, our payment for our efforts was truly priceless.

Chapter 31
Promises

Obviously, a day of playing cupid can be exhausting, so Barb and I slept in late the next day. We rolled out of bed about 9 a.m. and enjoyed a leisurely breakfast in our pajamas. After breakfast, I showered and dressed, but Barb stayed in her pajamas. This was shocking to me. I had never seen Barb spend an entire day in her pajamas, EVER! Not to be misunderstood. There is nothing wrong with hanging out in your PJs all day. It just wasn't part of Barb's personality. She was always up at sunrise, beautifully dressed, with her hair styled and shellacked with extra firm hairspray. Her nails were always polished, and her make-up was perfect. Each day at the crack of dawn, she was ready to face whatever the day had in store for her, and she always faced it with style and grace.

"What do you want to do today?" I asked her after I had showered and dressed.

"I just want to take it easy today," she answered. "I have a meeting with my cancer fundraising group tonight, and that's about it. Would you like to join me? There will be food at the meeting so that can be our evening meal."

"Yeah, sure," I responded. It would be interesting to see Barb in action at the meeting.

Barb was a self-proclaimed soap opera addict. Due to her recent chemotherapy schedule, she had been forced to record several weeks of her favorite daytime dramas. We spent the afternoon in her sunroom lounging in comfortable recliners, covered with cozy, handmade quilts, and munching on our favorite junk foods. It was a "hard knock" life we lived that day. It was also the perfect environment to talk.

"I noticed you had Mom's fake fur coat out in my bedroom. What up with that?" I asked. "Do you wear it?"

"Heavens no! I don't wear it," she laughed. "I have it out because it reminds me of her, and I've been doing a bit of spring housecleaning. I'm trying to decide what to do with it."

"Thank goodness you don't wear it," I confessed. "When Mom wore it, she always looked like a bear." We both laughed. "As for spring house cleaning, it's February! That's hardly spring."

"I know," Barb admitted. "I just felt like cleaning and getting everything organized."

That's strange, I thought to myself. Barb was clearly a type A personality. Every nook and cranny in her home was organized. Every aspect of her life was organized. I often wondered if her personality traits had developed from being the oldest sibling. She was a leader. She always had a mission and a purpose, and she got things done. In her professional life as entrepreneur and small business owner and in her personal life, she was a powerhouse. Maybe this was how she stayed organized, just a little bit at a time.

"You know how you said the fur coat reminds you of Mom. This room reminds me of Steve," I told her.

Our brother Steve was a carpenter who several years before his cancer diagnosis had converted

Barb's two-car garage into the sunroom we were currently enjoying. To be honest, it was the ultimate sunroom. One wall was completely glass. That area was filled with plants of various colors, shapes, and sizes. Intermixed with the plants were decorative items including birdhouses, watering cans, gardening tools, and signs with quaint quotes and sayings. At one time, the room housed a hot tub, and currently it had a large freshwater aquarium. Of course there was the large screen television, recliners, a love seat, and sofa. It was the centerpiece of Barb's home, and she easily spent ninety percent of her time there.

"Yeah, this room reminds me of Steve, too," she admitted as she gazed around the environment she and Steve had created together.

Our thoughts and conversation about Steve catapulted my mind back to the last time I saw my brother. At Christmas that year, Steve had shared with our family that his cancer was terminal. There was nothing else the doctors could do. There were no more surgeries, no more chemotherapy, and no more medications. He probably had a month or two to live.

I decided to take a week off from work in January to fly back to Iowa to spend time with Steve and to say good-bye. My mother had passed away a few months earlier, so I stayed with my dad knowing he would appreciate the company.

On my first full day back, Dad offered to drive me to Steve's home, which was about eight miles away. Dad drove. I rode shotgun in the passenger seat, and my three sisters piled into the backseat.

When we arrived, Steve was in the basement relaxing in his recliner. He was too weak to stand, so we took turns bending over him to give him a hug. After the hug fest, Dad and my sisters squeezed themselves onto the couch, and I took up residence in a nearby cushioned chair. Dad started the conversation with complaints about the cold weather and the possibility of an impending snowstorm. My sisters chimed in with accounts of winter weather from the past.

I didn't take part in the winter weather verbal exchange. I simply stared in disbelief at my relatives sitting on the couch discussing meteorological conditions. I hadn't traveled hundreds of miles to talk about the weather. There was clearly an elephant in the room that no one wanted to address. Steve was dying.

I wanted to talk to Steve about what he was going through and what he was feeling. Instead, we were discussing outdoor temperatures and precipitation. Although the conversation was mundane, the visit seemed to go by quickly, and soon we were hugging Steve good-bye.

I felt like I was back in high school when the next morning during breakfast, I asked Dad if I could borrow his car for the day.

"Sure, I'm not going anywhere," he replied. "Where are you going?"

"I'm going to visit Steve, but I want to go alone this time," I answered.

"I understand," Dad assured me as he handed me the keys to his car.

After breakfast, I drove to Steve's home in silence, internally praying I would know what to say to my beloved brother. Once I arrived, God seemed to take over the conversation. It all began with one simple question.

"Steve, are you afraid of dying," I asked.

"No," he responded. That was exactly what I had expected him to say. In my world he was Superman, and of course Superman isn't afraid of anything. Steve continued to explain his answer.

"I was afraid of dying at first," he continued. "Then I started experiencing something strange, but strange in a good way. It seemed to happen when I was right on the verge of being awake and falling asleep."

"I know what you mean. Tell me what happened," I encouraged him.

"It's hard to explain, but I'll try. It's like I no longer have a body, but I am floating in space. It's dark but not cold. There are rays of light, which are like stars but not really. Each light is a person who talks to me. Each person wants me to come with them telling me it is so peaceful where they exist. But each time this has happened, I tell them I'm not ready yet."

"Is Chad one of those people?" I asked him. Chad was Steve's son who had died in a motorcycle accident at the age of seventeen.

"No, I was hoping it would be Chad, but it wasn't."

"I'm sorry," I whispered trying to comfort my brother. "When Mom was sick, I read a book about dying written by a hospice nurse. She said many people would see a family member who was deceased, and that person would be their guide from this world to the next."

"I've heard that, too," Steve responded. "That's why I was hoping it would be Chad. I'd give anything to see him again."

"It could still happen," I assured him. "How many times have you experienced this situation?"

"Twice. Both times it was so peaceful and relaxing. I have to admit I was tempted to go with them, but I couldn't. I can't explain why. I just knew I wasn't ready."

"It will happen when the time is right."

"I know that is true, and that's why I'm not afraid anymore," he assured me.

At that moment, I felt as if a weight had been taken off my shoulders. I didn't want Steve to be afraid. If he had to die, I wanted him to die in peace. To tell the truth, I was afraid of dying until I heard Steve speak about his experiences. Now, not only his fear was gone, but so was mine.

I felt more satisfied with this conversation than I did with the one from the previous day. I had been watching my brother carefully and could tell he was getting tired. I hugged him good-bye and asked if I could visit him the next afternoon.

The next day we talked about God. Steve shared his belief that God is everywhere, not just in churches. He also explained he believed you could talk to God anywhere and at any time. You didn't always need to say a prayer but could talk to Him like He was a regular person. I must admit I liked

Steve's ideas which seemed so simple yet so brilliant.

At one point in the conversation, Steve said one of his friends had asked him why he didn't go to church on Sundays. His response was, "I'd rather be on a lake fishing and thinking about God than be in a church thinking about fishing." It made sense to me. It made me remember how very smart my Superman was.

The week continued in a similar fashion. I would arrive in the afternoon, and we would discuss whatever topic Steve wanted to explore. One day we reminisced about our favorite childhood memories. We shared funny stories about Mom, Dad, and our siblings. I laughed so hard that my stomach hurt and tears rolled down my face.

On my final visit, I asked Steve if he had any regrets. Was there anything he wanted to do that he had not been able to experience? He told me he wished he had traveled more. When I asked him where he would have gone, he replied, "Anywhere." I assured him if that was his only regret, then he had lived an awesome life. He agreed. He felt he had lived a wonderful life. He had a wife who was his soul mate and two sons who were his pride and joy. What more could a man ask for?

As our conversation was nearing an end, Steve had an interesting request.

"I want you to promise me something," he began. "Promise me you will have a colonoscopy as soon as you can. Everyone in our family needs to be tested. You are supposed to have your first one at age fifty, but look at me, I'm never going to make it to age fifty."

He was right. He was always right. The request was so Steve-like. I had returned home to visit and comfort him but in the end he turned the tables and made the situation to be about me. He was always the protective big brother looking out for his little sister. Of course, I agreed to his request.

It was hard to leave that day knowing it would be the last time I would see or touch my big brother in this life. Steve and I both rose from our chairs in order to hug each other. Our embrace lasted several minutes, neither one of us wanting to let go. Finally,

I whispered in his ear, "I love you, Steve. You are my Superman." He squeezed me as tightly as he could. As I let him go, I saw tears in his eyes, and I knew he couldn't speak. Maybe we had spoken enough over the past week. Maybe this was a situation in which no words were necessary. I squeezed his hand, said good-bye, and left. I knew I could not look back for fear I would run back to hug him again. I knew it was time to let go.

I cried all the way back to Dad's house. The tears rolled down my face in salty streams. At times, it was difficult to see the highway. My eyes were blurry, and memories of Steve flashed through my imagination. I tried to imagine life without Steve, but it wasn't in my realm of thinking. When I reached my parents' home, I parked the car in the garage, and scurried to my bedroom. I didn't want Dad to see my tear stained face. He never did well with crying.

I flew back to Colorado the following day. Steve joined the people of the twinkling lights in their peaceful existence on February 23rd, 1999. He must have known the time was right. I convinced my doctor to allow me to have a colonoscopy at the age of thirty-eight. While I was being tested, I decided to also have a mammogram even though I wasn't forty years old yet. My doctors continued to monitor a suspicious spot on my right breast, until eventually, I was diagnosed with breast cancer. Just as the mythical Superman saved the lives of many people, I credit my Superman with saving mine.

Sitting in the sunroom that Steve built, being alone with Barb as she lounged in her recliner, thinking of Steve's, Barb's, and my journey with cancer made me have the courage to make an important request of Barb.

"Barb, let's promise each other that every time we are together, we will treat it like it is our last time to ever be together," I began. "Let's be truthful and honest with each other. Let's make the time we have together really count, and let's always say the words 'I love you' before we part."

"I can promise that," Barb said. "I'm just wondering why you are asking me this now?"

"I'm not saying this because I think either one of us is going to die from cancer," I explained. "I was just thinking about Steve and Chad. It made me realize how uncertain life is. Not to be morbid or anything, but on any given day, one of us could be run over by a truck. BAM! In a split second one of us could be road kill."

"That's funny, but it's not funny," Barb said. Then after a few moments of deep thought she added, "I can make that promise. I promise that each time we are together we will treat it like it's our last time together." Years later, I realize the importance of those promises. My promise to Steve actually saved my life, while my promise to Barb taught me how to live it.

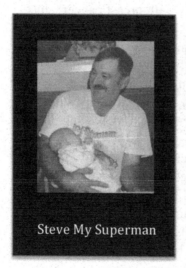

Steve My Superman

Barb The Warrior Chick

Chapter 32
I Hope You Dance

"This is my baby sister. She's a breast cancer survivor." This is how Barb introduced me to each person attending the cancer fundraising meeting. In return, each person would tell me their name, the type of cancer they had been diagnosed with, and how many years they had been cancer free. It was as if the cancer type and how many years they had been cancer free had become part of their identity. Perhaps this information was relevant due to the environment. After all, we were at a cancer fundraising meeting. One thing for sure was hearing how many years each person had been free of cancer was very encouraging to me. I was also enlightened by the fact that although each individual's personal battle with cancer was over, their battles with cancer as a whole would continue until the dreaded disease was eradicated from the face of the planet. Even though they were cancer free, they had committed themselves to raising money to find the cure so the world would be cancer free. That was truly amazing. Certainly, I was in the company of warriors and heroes.

Barb had been a leader in this organization for several years. After her colon cancer diagnosis, she had remained a member but had stepped down from a leadership role in order to concentrate on her own health. Barb had been a mentor to me throughout my cancer journey, and clearly by the vibe in the room, she was a mentor to many other people as well. In fact, she had the mentor role down to a

271

fine-tuned art form. She never portrayed herself as a know-it-all or expert, but more of a trusted, wise, resource, and friend.

After circulating around the room to socialize, we grabbed a few slices of pizza, and Barb strategically sat at a table in the front of the room. Soon the meeting began. There was a report regarding membership from the secretary, as well as a finance report from the treasurer. Next up was the president. She spoke about the three major fundraisers, which were going to occur in the next several months. These were the daffodil sales, a golf tournament, and the granddaddy of them all, the Relay for Life in June. "Isn't that how we usually do this, Barb?" inquired the president after she spoke about each event.

Of course, Barb would answer the questions and interject a few helpful hints in her kind, matter of fact manner. It was clear she was their rock, their go to person, but it was also clear Barb was letting go, training them to lead on their own within the structure of her guidance.

I had never been so proud of my big sister as I was that night. It was obvious how the members of the group respected Barb as a leader, but also how much they truly loved her as a person. Love and respect, what more could any person ask or wish for?

On the drive back to her home that evening, we discussed the Relay for Life in June. The tone in Barb's voice was proof of the excitement she felt about the relay teams and the fund raising activities. As she shared, the pace of her speech increased. I listened with pure admiration. I loved to see her in her warrior chick mode. Unfortunately, I had to be the one to put the brakes on the positivity train.

"I'll be coming back to Iowa for the Fourth of July for my class reunion," I told her. "Then in August I'll be back for the wedding (our niece was getting married)."

"That will be great," she responded.

"But the not so great part is because I'll be back in July and August, I don't think I can swing coming back in June for the Relay for Life," I added.

"That's okay," she assured me as she flashed me a smile. "There's always next year."

There's always another day, another year, and for the most part that is true, but sometimes it isn't. I was glad I had returned home that year to help with the Valentine's Day deliveries because it ended up being the last Valentine's Day my niece owned the flower shop. In the next few months, she sold her business and followed her heart to a new career. The entire situation reminded me of the saying "Carpe Diem" or seize the day. I had made the right choice in coming to Iowa to help deliver the gifts of love instead of putting it off yet another year. Little did I know, it was a once in a lifetime opportunity and certainly a memorable one.

Even though I couldn't attend the Relay for Life in Iowa, Barb continued her tradition of sending me a t-shirt from the event. My husband and son joined me on the trip to my hometown in July. Our kids loved staying at Barb's home because she spoiled them with treats, candy, love, and attention. What human being doesn't love that?

I enjoyed spending time with my classmates. With a class of just over fifty people, you are more like family members rather than classmates. As a class, we created a float for the Fourth of July parade and actually won a small prize for our efforts. Besides the float building, we found time to eat, drink, and socialize. While I appreciated the time I was able to spend with my classmates, I didn't want to neglect Barb.

"What would you like to do during the Fourth of July celebration?" I asked her one evening.

"I would really like to go to the street dance," she told me. This was a shock because I had never seen Barb dance. My reaction must have shown on my face because she added," The band that is playing is supposed to be really good, and I just want to see who will be at the dance."

I translated this into meaning we would go to the dance, sit at a table, enjoy a few drinks, and talk to a lot of people because Barb was the ultimate social butterfly. If that was what Barb wanted to do, that was okay with me. It actually sounded like a fun evening.

The sun was setting when Barb and I headed to the street dance. In a town of eight hundred people, a side street was blocked off to became the stage and the dance floor. When we arrived at the entrance, there was a cover charge. As I reached into my purse to retrieve my billfold, Barb said, "Let's just wait out here for a while before we pay. I want to hear the band and see who comes."

"That's fine with me," I assured her.

Soon we became the official "Wal-Mart greeters." We stood at the gate, and Barb talked to everyone who entered. Many people mistook us for the gatekeepers, and tried to hand us money for the cover charge. Finally after an hour, I said, "Barb, let's go in. I'll pay for the cover charge. I want to sit down and have a drink." But my request wasn't granted.

Barb loved to talk. Often when she called me, it wasn't truly a conversation. She would talk, and I would listen. There really wasn't a true exchange of words.

Two hours later, we decided to leave the dance and return to her home. We never did make it past the entrance gate, and that was our street dance experience. Barb had a wonderful evening, loving every minute of the night, and that was all that mattered.

In mid August, I returned to Iowa for our niece's wedding. As always, I stayed at Barb's home. Barb and I had a tradition of sending each other gift cards to our favorite clothing store for our birthdays. When we were together, we would show each other what we had purchased with the gift cards and rave about each other's good taste. We were in the middle of our fashion show, when Barb confided in me.

"You know, I just can't seem to kick the cancer this time," she said. "No matter what I do or try, it just keeps coming back."

This is a pivotal point for anyone who has ever been on the outside looking into the life of a cancer patient. You don't want to blow it off by saying it's going to be fine, or it's going to be okay, because that's what everybody says to a cancer patient. It's the standard answer, and as a cancer patient myself, I knew this was true. When someone tells you it's going to be okay, it is not helpful. No one knows it is going to be okay. But saying nothing would be even worse. I think in this situation you need to be able to read or infer what the person is really saying to you. Do they simply want you to listen? Do they want you to respond, but respond authentically and not with the standard "canned" answer. I took a moment to think, to read between the lines, to translate what Barb was saying to me. I found it ironic that I was afraid my cancer would come back, while she was afraid her cancer would never leave, but the outcome was the same. We were both afraid that cancer would end our lives. What would I have wanted someone to say to me in this situation?

"I know I've said this before, but I've come to the realization that none of us know how our lives will end. Look what happened to Chad." Chad was our nephew who had unexpectedly died at the age of seventeen in a motorcycle accident. "One of us could be struck by lightning or hit by a car or . . ."

"Die from cancer," Barb finished my sentence.

"Or die from cancer," I repeated. "I don't know why you, me, Dad, and Steve ended up having cancer. It just appears to be luck of the draw."

"Yeah, bad luck," Barb added.

"No kidding. I mean we seemed to be fairly healthy people then BAM out of nowhere we each get hit with a cancer diagnosis," I told her. "Here is one thing I do know. I treat every day like it is my last. I go on trips. I hang out with my favorite people. I read the books that I've always wanted to read. If I have to do some mundane tasks, then at least I do them with joy and make the experiences fun. Actually, you are the one that taught me how cancer changes your life. It forces you to see life with a whole new perspective."

"Sometimes in life it's easier to give advice to someone else rather than to take that advice yourself," she admitted.

"It's pretty good advice," I told her. "You should listen to yourself. In the meantime, we have a wedding to get ready for. Let's go 'beautify' ourselves."

When Barb emerged from our primping session, she looked like a million bucks. Her textured, royal blue sheath dress ended slightly below her knees. Matching earrings and understated shoes completed the classy, sophisticated look, which was reminiscent of Audrey Hepburn's style.

I, on the other hand, had chosen a more casual look with a silky, colorful blouse and a pair of black dress pants. I had dressed more for the wedding dance rather than the wedding ceremony. I had learned from experience that you can't get down and get funky while wearing pantyhose.

Dancing was an interesting phenomenon in our family. Our parents loved to dance. In fact, they went out dancing with their friends on Saturday nights. They knew how to polka, waltz, and fox trot, but they also loved to move spontaneously to the music. They simply loved dancing. Out of the six children in our family, Jan, Mary, and I loved to dance; Barb and our two brothers, Steve and Kevin, not so much.

The wedding ceremony was beautiful. What wedding isn't? Glancing around the church I saw the loved filled faces of my siblings, their spouses, their grown children, our favorite cousins, and an assortment of treasured relatives. Everyone knows weddings are about love, but more than just the romantic love between the bride and the groom. There is the love that is shared by all the guests. It is a bond, a relationship between everyone who is invited. I looked down at the goose bumps on my arms. Yep, love does that to you. It gives you goose bumps, no matter what kind of love it is.

Figuring out how to transport everyone to the wedding reception venue was somewhat of a Chinese fire drill in the church parking lot. Everyone piled into the available cars. Suddenly a child would realize he or she wanted to ride with a favorite cousin, aunt or uncle, and spontaneously popped out of one car into another. Fortunately, we all arrived at the reception venue safe and sound.

After a few shots from the bar, courtesy of my sister Mary, and a delicious, gourmet meal, the dance began. Of course, the festivities started with the bride and groom's first dance as man and wife. I glanced down at my arms. Yep, goose bumps. My brother Kevin danced with his daughter, the bride. Goose bumps and tears. The groom danced with his mother. Goose bumps and more tears.

When the guests were invited onto the dance floor, Jan, Mary, and I were quick to leave our table to claim a section of prime real estate on the dance floor. The three of us were of the mindset that you really didn't need to have a dance partner. We just enjoyed the music, bobbing and swaying along with the rhythm and beat of each song, clapping our hands and laughing in celebration of the moment. Mom and Dad would have been proud.

Periodically, we would return to the table with sweat dripping down our temples to refresh ourselves with frosty glasses of ice water or sparkling soda. During our first break, we tried to convince Barb to join us.

"Carl (Barb's colostomy) doesn't like to dance," she told us. The first few notes of the song "Happy" by Pharrell Williams interrupted our conversation.

"That's my favorite song!" Mary screamed with delight. "Let's go dance!" she exclaimed as she dragged Jan and I onto the dance floor, leaving Barb with the rest of the non-dancing relatives.

My body may have been on the dance floor moving and grooving to the music, but my heart was back at the table with Barb. Over the last several months, the two of us had shared conversations regarding living each day of life as if it were your last. It's one thing to pay lip service to the concept, and another to actually do it. It's like the old saying, "Actions speak louder than words." I wasn't going to let this evening be a repeat of the street dance where we spent the night being spectators at the gate. If it was true that Barb's cancer wasn't under control and maybe it never would be, then she needed to dance. She needed to stop being a spectator and start being a participant. That evening dancing was a metaphor, a symbol of living. I wanted to go back to the table and scream at Barb, "Dance! Live! Live! Live! Do it now before it's too late!" But that wasn't going to accomplish anything other than to make her mad, so I went to Plan B. After the song "Happy" ended, I made my way to the disc jockey.

"Could you play the song 'We Are Family' by Sister Sledge?" I asked him.

"Of course, I love that song," he replied. "I have a couple songs already queued up, and that will give me a few minutes to find it, but it will be right up."

"Fantastic!" I told him. "You are the 'bomb!'" I've found it never hurts to compliment the disc jockey at a dance then basically you can get any song played that your heart desires. I scurried off to the table in order to wait for my "evil" plan to unfold.

Two songs and two glasses of ice water later, the song "We Are Family" started to play. Of course Mary and Jan loved that song and were drawn to the dance floor like moths to a porch light.

"Come on, Barb. They are playing our song. Let's go dance," I enticed her.

"I told you Carl doesn't like to dance," she explained.

"Since when have you let Carl tell you what you can and cannot do?" I asked. "I'm not taking no for an answer this time, Barb. We're going to dance."

Reluctantly, she stood up, and that was all I needed. I just needed her to get out of her chair, and the rest would be a piece of cake, in this case a piece of wedding cake.

Mary and Jan were already getting down on the dance floor, so Barb and I joined them forming a circle. In a matter of seconds, several of our nieces increased the size of our dancing circle. The circle continued to grow as more relatives joined our celebration. When the words of the chorus "We are family. I've got all my sisters and me!" echoed through the dance hall, we pumped our right fists into the air and sang along as if exclaiming a battle cry. For me, it was a battle cry for Barb, "Live, Barb, live! Live, my beloved sister! Don't leave me, now! I need you! I've always needed you. I've needed you since the day I was born. My wish for you, dear sister, is dance. I hope you dance."

Siblings at Wedding Dance

Chapter 33
I'm Going Home

Barb did dance the night of the wedding dance. In fact, we had a hard time getting her to stop. I had never seen her dance like that in my entire life. She danced. She laughed. She lived. She was happy. I was happy, very happy.

I have been to enough dances to know that disc jockeys play the song "YMCA" by the Village People for one of two reasons. When the party is starting to drag a little, you just pop on that song and WHAM! Everyone is instantly regenerated with a new level of energy and enthusiasm. The song is also used to gauge if the end of the party is near. When people are too tired or too tipsy to correctly form the letters Y-M-C-A with their bodies, then you know it is time to call it quits. Such was the case with our brother-in-law, Ron. He could not correctly form one letter from the song, not even the "Y". This was clearly an indication it was time to call it a night and go home.

Just like a song, every dance needs to have a crescendo before it ends. In this case, the crescendo was the song "What a Wonderful World" sung by Louis Armstrong. Everyone in the room, including the non-dancers at the tables, joined us to form a huge circle on the dance floor. With my sisters, including Barb, beside me, our arms intertwined around each other's shoulders, swaying to the music, I realized it is a wonderful world if we only take the time to see it, to appreciate it, to live in it with every ounce of our being. Life is good. We just need to take the opportunity to realize that.

It was a tradition in the groom's family to end a wedding dance with the songs "Piano Man" by Billy Joel and "Sweet Caroline" sung by Neil Diamond. We stayed in the gigantic circle we had created, swaying to the music and singing the lyrics. I had just met the groom's family on this day, but if they had the tradition of ending wedding dances with the song "Piano Man," I loved them already. We had experienced a wonderful day. We had celebrated love. We had enjoyed being together. Barb had danced, really danced. It couldn't get any better than that.

I returned to our home near Colorado Springs, but another celebration was brewing back in Iowa. Barb's birthday was approaching at the end of September, and it was going to be a big one, seventy years young! Her daughter-in-law was planning a wonderful surprise party for the entire community to enjoy. As much as my spirit wanted to return home for the party, my budget said no way. Whether I drove or flew, each time I returned to Iowa it cost several hundred dollars. Usually, I made the trip once a year. This year, I had already made the trip home in February, July, and August. Going back one more time in September just wasn't in the cards, but I was determined to make the best of the situation. I selected the most gorgeous bouquet of cut flowers I could find on-line and requested the delivery to be on the exact date of Barb's birthday. I always find flowers are something most women don't purchase for themselves, but love receiving. They are beautiful and decadent. I called Barb the evening of her party when I knew the festivities were over.

"How was your surprise party?" I started the conversation.

"It was fabulous! It really couldn't have been any better," she said then she went on to describe her favorite gifts, and people who attended that she hadn't seen in many years. "I'm just so tired," she concluded. "I'm so very tired."

She thanked me for the flowers, stating how much she enjoyed them. We talked briefly about appreciating each birthday we have been given, especially this milestone one.

"Love you, Sis," I proclaimed, ending the conversation.

"I love you, too," Barb whispered.

Little did any of us know the birthday party would be Barb's last hurrah. She was more than tired. She was exhausted. The cancer was spreading throughout her body faster than chemotherapy chemicals could kill the rogue cells.

Barb lived alone, and there was concern she was too weak to care for herself. The decision was made that she would check into the local nursing home. It was the nursing home she and her husband had owned for several years before selling it to a corporation. Barb handled most of the finances for the business including payroll, accounts receivable, accounts payable, taxes . . . the whole ball of wax. She had the luxury of driving to work or walking to work because the care center was next to her home on a dead end street of all places.

Needless to say, Barb was in good hands. Several employees were still there who worked with and loved Barb. They treated her with the same kindness she had shared with them. Ironically, her room had the most beautiful view of her home. I'm sure very few people could say they had a view of their home from their care center room.

After the sale of the care center to the corporation, the halls had been designated as wings. There was the Alzheimer's wing, the regular care wing, the rehab wing, and an entire new section had been built for assisted living.

Shortly after she moved in, I called Barb. She was quick to explain she was in the rehab wing, and she was only going to stay long enough to regain her strength and move back to her home.

"I'm going home. That's my goal. I'm going back to my home," she would tell me each time I called.

After several weeks, when I called her cell phone, she didn't answer. This concerned me, so I began dialing the front desk number. "Barb's sleeping, and she doesn't want to be disturbed," was the response I would receive each time I called.

"Did you tell her it was Pam?" I questioned. Barb didn't want to talk to me? *How could that be? I was her baby sister, the one she had coddled and spoiled since birth.* Maybe my ego had kicked into overdrive, but if Barb didn't want to talk to me and didn't return my calls, then something was wrong.

After several weeks of this pattern, I called my number one partner in crime, my sister Mary. I explained the situation to her and voiced my concern. I asked her to personally go to the care center to find out exactly what was happening.

"Jan and I have already been to the care center," Mary confided. "The same thing was happening to us. When we would call, they told us she was sleeping and didn't want to be disturbed. It kept happening over and over so Jan and I went there to visit, and they wouldn't let us in her room. It was the same thing. She was sleeping and didn't want to be disturbed."

"Something is wrong, Mary. I just know it. I can feel it." I pleaded.

I knew in my heart I needed to go home, to go back to Iowa to find out what was going on, but the logical part of me knew I needed to stay in Colorado. One of our children was facing a life or death health issue. My new job had become dealing with the health insurance company and searching out medical professionals to save my child's life. I couldn't see how I could continue that battle from Iowa.

I had called Mary for a reason. We had been partners in crime in several situations, and I knew I could count on her to get things done, but we were partners so I had every intention of pulling my weight.

"How about you call Robb (Barb's only child), and I'll call Joy (our niece who was a hospice nurse)? Let's see what we can find out," I suggested to Mary.

"Sounds good," she agreed.

Joy lived in Illinois. We would text one another with regular, everyday stuff, but when we called each other, it meant something bad had happened. I hated to admit it, but it was true.

I'm sure my name popped up on Joy's caller ID, so she answered her phone, "What's up? Who died?"

"Nobody died," I responded. "I'm worried about Barb, and I need your professional opinion about the situation," I blurted out without even asking about how she or her kids were. I explained I had been trying to call Barb but was constantly told she was asleep and didn't want to be disturbed. Mary and Jan had experienced the same situation, even when they went to the care center in person.

"The nurses there are not lying to you. Barb is probably sleeping a lot because her body is shutting down," Joy began.

"What do you mean shutting down?" I asked, even though I knew what Joy meant, I wanted to hear her say it out loud, plain, and clear.

"Barb is dying, Pam," Joy said. "I've seen this many times at work. Her body is shutting down. She's preparing to die, not only physically, but also she is letting go of all of you. It's a transition from this life to the next."

"How long?" was all I could say.

"I have no way of telling without seeing her. Her doctor knows. She knows, but knowing Barb, she's not going to tell anyone. She is always taking care of everybody. She doesn't want to burden us with that information," Joy explained. Joy was right. She knew Barb so well. We all did. I thanked Joy then told her I loved and missed her like I always did.

A call to Mary revealed she had uncovered the same information from Robb. My dilemma now was whether to stay to care for my sick child or to return home to say my last good-bye to my terminally ill sister. I couldn't make that decision on the spot. I needed at least a couple of days to decide what to do. Life eventually made the decision for me.

My husband and I were on our way to the emergency room. He was driving well over the speed limit, and I was in the backseat holding on to our child as tight as I could. My phone rang, and I felt the need to answer it. It was Barb's daughter-in-law.

"Pam, Barb doesn't have much longer to live," she sobbed. "If you want to say good-bye to her, you need to come home now."

"I can't," I said. Then I went on to explain the situation we were experiencing to her. "We are headed to the emergency room, and I expect it will lead to an extended hospital stay. I can't leave now."

"I understand. You do what you have to do," she said. "I just wanted you to know what is going on here."

"I thank you for that," I told her. "Sometimes being the one who lives miles away means I'm out of the loop." She called me several times that evening to update me on Barb's condition and to check in with us as to what was happening in our situation.

The next morning, the wife of Barb's grandson called me.

"It's happening now, Pam," she sobbed. "We are all with her, surrounding her bed and holding her hands. She is comatose, and her breathing is shallow. I can hold the phone up to her ear if you want to say good-bye."

It was as if my mind was on autopilot. "No, Barb and I have already said our good-byes. We made a promise to each other that we would treat every good-bye like it was our last," I told her. Somehow telling Barb good-bye when she was in a coma seemed fake to me. I had told her good-bye when she was coherent, when it counted the most. It was time to let go. Barb was going home just like she said she was going to, but it wasn't to her home on the lot next to the nursing home. It was to our heavenly home to be with God our Father. That was so like Barb. If she said something was going to happen, it was going to happen one way or another. She was a kickass; get things done, kind of warrior chick.

On November 29, 2014, she joined our parents, our nephew Chad, and our brother Steve in the realm of "beckoning souls" that Steve had described. She was at peace. She was home.

Pam, Kendall (Barb's Great Granddaughter) and Barb

Chapter 34
Life and Death Lessons

Barb had purchased her cemetery plot and a beautiful headstone, but other than that, she had not left any instructions regarding her funeral. Her son and his family decided to delay her memorial service in order to make the arrangements according to what they thought she would have liked and appreciated. This decision gave them time to arrange and organize the service, deal with their grief, and live through their first Christmas without Barb.

I was grateful for the time as well. My family was able to use the time for the healing of our child and for the healing of our emotions from the crisis we had recently experienced. For the time being, we were on the path of recovery, but there would be several more years of struggle and turmoil regarding our child's health. The struggle and turmoil was regarding physical and mental ailments, but also with the interactions with the health insurance company. Between co-pays and hospital stays, our emergency fund had been depleted once again. This time there would be no magical, forgotten insurance policy to reimburse the fund. The money was gone.

Christmas without Barb was nothingness. There wasn't a beautiful Christmas card that arrived from her in the mail to brighten our spirits. There were no gifts, which she had chosen especially for each person. There were no photos of her home decorated both inside and out for the holidays. Christmas that year was just plain nothingness.

I began to think about the journey Barb and I had been on. Our roles were interchangeable. First, she was the cancer patient who had been diagnosed with melanoma, and I was the supportive sister. Then I became the cancer patient, and she was the supportive sister. In the end, we were both cancer patients, but we were more than supportive sisters, through our journey, we had become soul mates.

As humans, I believe we often forget to think about the fact that our lives are a journey, and every journey has a destination, an end. We often spend time and effort planning our lives in terms of who we love, where we live, and what we do. But do we plan for what will happen once we reach our destinations?

I don't think any of us can argue with the fact that the end of life's journey is death. Because there is uncertainty about what the afterlife will be like, many people find death to be frightening. This fear leads people to deny the inevitable, to deny that death even exists. Denial may delay an event, but it never stops it from happening. Fortunately, for all of us, denial can be replaced by faith. If we truly believe God has a life waiting for us after death, and it is more wonderful than anything our mere mortal minds can imagine, then what do we have to fear?

I don't know if Barb ever reached this level of faith. Only Barb knew the answer to that question. Clearly, she hadn't planned for the end of her earthly journey. In my conversations with her, right up to the end of her life, she refused to talk about

291

dying. The lesson I learned through this process was that dying is as individual as living. As a loving, supportive person who is part of the life of someone who is terminally ill, I believe we need to respect that person's wishes regarding death. As difficult as that may be, it is part of loving them.

My dad's idea of death was to fall asleep and not wake up. Although he feared death, he had every detail of his funeral planned right down to the meal of scalloped potatoes and ham to be served after the graveside ceremony. My brother Steve wanted to die in the comfort of his own home, and that is exactly what he did. Barb denied the fact that she was dying, and that's okay, too. Her denial was actually a testament to her positive thinking. As far as she was concerned, she was in the rehab wing of the care center for a reason. She was going home.

The lessons to be learned here are simple and yet intertwined. Everything is unique to each individual. There is not a right or wrong way to do something. There is only that person's way, which fits their life, their personality, their environment, their situation, and their relationship with God. There is no right way to travel the cancer journey, whether you are the patient or someone who loves a patient. There is no right way to live your life, and there is no right way to die.

When it came time for Barb's memorial service, my husband and kids were still in school, so I made the pilgrimage back to the Midwest alone. Barb's home was cold, dark, and deserted. It was merely a wooden structure without her. Barb's personality and magic were what made her house a home. Just like Christmas, her home was now nothingness so I opted to stay at my sister Mary's house.

The memorial service was absolutely perfect. Barb's son and his family did an exquisite job attending to every detail of the ceremony so that it reflected Barb's personality. The urn, which held her ashes, was decorated with plant designs as a tribute to her love of gardening. Photos of Barb's life adorned the entrance of the funeral home, bringing back fond memories for all of the guests. Time was set-aside for people to share memories and stories of Barb. Just like her life, this was a time for both laughter and tears.

The most touching aspect of the service was everyone was welcome to attend, and judging by the line outside of the funeral home, many people from the community did attend. The small town girl with a high school education had grown up to become an entrepreneur who was not only a cornerstone of the community, but also a beloved friend to many people. She and her husband had owned and operated the local nursing home, the bowling alley, an auto parts store, a liquor store, a retail furniture business, and a pizza restaurant. It was Barb's friendly, outgoing personality, her spunk and genuine interest in people and their lives that gave each business they owned a bit of character, and an essence of family and community. Without Barb's magic, those businesses would have been just buildings.

I think in their hearts the people in the town knew this. It was unwritten, unspoken, but undeniable. So they came to share their stories, their laughter, their friendship, and their respect as a tribute to one of their community members. Barb had touched their lives, making them feel special, and for that, they were grateful.

At the end of the service as people passed through the receiving line to share their condolences, I realized the diversity of her friends. Her friends from the bowling alley were a jovial, fun-loving bunch with endless humorous stories to tell about Barb the bowler. Her colleagues from the nursing home were the epitome of compassion, kindness, and empathy. Obviously, those characteristics were prerequisites to be in the profession of caring for others. Then there were her kindred spirits from her cancer fundraising group. This group of warriors and heroes were the life of the party because due to the cancer curve life had thrown them; they had a whole new outlook on life. The hilarious, zany stories they shared about Barb were endless, but the depth of their sorrow regarding her death was infinite as well. They were a true family, and they had lost a beloved family member. Barb's death was a reminder that any one of them could be in her place. Any one of them could have a recurrence of the deadly disease. Her death was an "in your face" reminder of each person's mortality.

It was a cold, winter night outside when the last guest left the memorial service. Barb's son and his family were exhausted and had left. Mary and I were doing a bit of last minute clean up, when the funeral home director approached us carrying Barb's urn.

"I was wondering, what should I do with Barb?" he asked as he nodded his head in the direction of the urn.

I had no idea, so I looked to Mary for the answer.

"Since it's the middle of winter, her family is going to wait until spring to place her remains in her gravesite," Mary responded. "Her son has already left so I don't know what to tell you."

"I'll be happy to take Barb home with me," he stated nonchalantly as if this was a common situation in his profession. "She'll have a place of honor on my fireplace mantle. I'll take good care of her until spring," he added. "She was a sweet lady, and I would be honored to do that for her."

Of course, I should have known the funeral director was a friend of Barb's. That made sense, perfect sense. She had a friendship with everyone within a twenty-mile radius.

With the memorial service over, I knew it was time to return to my home in Colorado, but I also knew there was one more thing I needed to do in order to have a sense of closure. So the following day, I called Barb's son.

"Robb, I'd like to go to Barb's house to say my final good-byes, if you don't mind," I asked him over the phone.

"Sure, no problem. Just come to our house to get the key," he told me.

"I just want to sit in her recliner in the sunroom. It was always her favorite place. If I could do that, I think I would feel closer to her," I explained.

There was a hesitation. I didn't hear Robb's voice for an extended period of time, but it wasn't an uncomfortable silence.

"The chair isn't there," he said slowly. "I took it to the nursing home when she moved in there, and I didn't bring it back."

This was one of those times in life when I felt I needed to read between the lines and interpret what Robb was really saying. Barb's recliner was her trademark. It was her favorite place. She watched soap operas and NASCAR races from that chair. She entertained guests and talked to her friends on the phone from that chair. She could see her garden, and watch the birds and the wildlife in her yard from that chair. While the chair brought me comfort and made me feel closer to Barb, it did the exact opposite for Robb. It was a physical reminder that his mother was gone. She would never sit in that chair again. When he looked at it he saw a huge, gaping hole in his life. When I looked at the recliner, I saw Barb, and I relived the memories we had shared. I was reminded of the fact that just as people live their lives in their own ways, people need to grieve in their own ways as well.

"That's okay," I told Robb. "Don't worry about it. You do what you've got to do. Can I still go to the house?"

"Yeah, sure," he rebounded. "Just stop by and get the key."

Borrowing Mary's car for transportation, I went that evening. The entrance to Barb's house was her gorgeous sunroom. It truly was the epicenter of her home. She could have easily lived in just that room.

The rest of the rooms in the house were mere accessories.

I flipped on the lights. My eyes were immediately drawn to the direction of her recliner. I almost expected Barb to be sitting there poised to ask me, "What are you doing here?"

The only reminder of the recliner was the indentations in the carpet where the chair had sat for years, if not decades. I walked up the steps to the kitchen to turn on the lights. Soon every light in the house was on, but it still felt dark and gloomy without Barb to light the dreary scene.

I didn't waste any time. I had a mission. I headed to what I referred to as "my room." When I arrived, I sat on the edge of the bed. It was time for reflection.

I thought of the many happy times I had spent in the room as a young girl playing with the dolls and stuffed animals, which inhabited the space. When I was a little girl staying with Barb, it meant fun, working in Barb's garden, eating contraband candy Mother would never let me consume, and just the joy of being with Barb.

As a teenager, I remembered sitting on the edge of that bed spilling my guts to Barb, telling her that Mom and Dad just didn't understand me. Little did I know at that time, I didn't even understand myself. She had placed her arm around me and comforted me saying, "That's just part of growing up. It's going to be okay." I believed her. I always believed her. She was my older sister, my second mother, my mentor, and my friend. Why wouldn't I believe her?

I remembered being a young woman and confiding in her that I wanted to leave our hometown to venture out into the world, to go to college, to have a career, to meet new people, to experience different ideas, to have some adventure in my life. She encouraged me to follow my dreams, and she did everything she could to help me on my journey whether it was borrowing her car or giving me a few words of encouragement handwritten in a card. She was always there for me no matter what stage of life I was struggling through.

The house held so much history for me. Memories of my life ran through my imagination like a movie on a theater screen. A feeling of serenity washed over me. Perhaps my mission here was complete, so I decided to circulate through the house, saying my last good-byes, and shutting off the lights.

When I arrived at the kitchen, I spotted a pile of dirty dishes in the sink. Robb and his family had been working on packing Barb's belongings for many weeks. I was sure they had eaten meals and snacks and had either forgotten to clean up or were too tired to do the dishes. I decided to do a good deed and quickly wash them.

As the sink began to fill with warm water, and the suds began to rise like a white, fluffy cloud, I thought of all the times Barb and I had stood at this very spot doing the dishes together. Barb never owned a dishwasher. I would often ask her why she didn't have such a modern day appliance that would make her life easier.

"I don't have room for a dishwasher," she would reply. "Besides, it's just me now. I don't dirty that many dishes."

At this moment in time, I was glad Barb never had a dishwasher because if she did, I would have missed out on so many meaningful conversations with her. She would always wash. I would always dry and put the dishes away. I knew every inch of her kitchen as if it were my own. As the dishes were cleaned, dried, and returned to their places in the cupboards, we solved all of the world's problems. We discussed the idiosyncrasies of men, the challenges of raising children, the frustrations of being a woman in a man's world, and lately what we could do as individuals to stop the spread of cancer.

Thinking of the word cancer tripped a trigger in my brain. It unlocked a gate in my inner being. All the anger and hostility I had stored there for years came rushing out, unleashed, unbridled, and uncontrolled.

Damn you, cancer! Why did you have to take Barb from me? Why did you take her away from all the people who cared about her and who needed her? Her work here on Earth wasn't finished. Why did you have to take Steve? He was such a kind, gentle, thoughtful soul. He was my quiet genius, my Superman. Why did you have to torture Dad? Not with one type of cancer, but two. Just like Barb. Wasn't one battle with cancer enough? Why me? It didn't bother me that I was diagnosed with cancer as much as the fact that I felt my diagnosis frightened the kids at school. That just wasn't fair.

I placed my head down on the edge of the sink and sobbed. My body was shaking in ebbs and waves of sorrow, my stomach muscles contracting, the tears falling down and splashing on the tops of my shoes.

As we all know, the questions in life always come before the answers. At that moment, my entire being was filled not only with sorrow, but with a multitude of unanswered questions.

Enough with the crying, I told myself. Barb would have given me a swift kick to the behind and sent me on my way. I dried my eyes with my shirtsleeves since my hands were covered with dishwater and soapsuds. I reached into the sink to remove the plug so the water could drain, and that's when it hit me. The water NEVER drained from this sink, at least not without the help of a plunger. Over the years, the situation had gone from bad to worse. At first, it was just slow and as the situation deteriorated, it wouldn't drain at all. Barb would retrieve the plunger and use it until she was exhausted then it was my turn to use the primitive plumbing tool. The entire time Barb would be swearing, "This #?!* sink!" We would both laugh hysterically throughout the entire ordeal.

"Why don't you call a plumber and get this fixed?" I would ask her.

"What fun would that be?" she insisted. "Look at us. Look at how we are laughing and how much fun we are having." She was right. She was always right.

As I went to retrieve the plunger from its secret hiding place, I realized Barb wasn't physically with me in the kitchen that night, but I knew she was watching over me just like she always did.

As I pushed on the plunger with all of my body weight then released it to create a powerful suction, I felt whatever was blocking the pipe below let go. A gurgling sound escaped from the sink as the water was sucked down the drain in a swirling hurricane-like motion. Suddenly, I realized that #?!* plugged sink was a metaphor for my life. Just like the clog in the sink had prevented the water from draining, my anger and hostility regarding cancer, and its attack on my family members, had prevented me from living life to its fullest. Just as the clog in the sink was gone, I considered my crying tantrum to be the catalyst, which removed my anger and sorrow. I was no longer going to focus on the questions. I was going to focus on the answers. I was going to let the water flow.

As I finished shutting off the lights, I felt the memories of my life come floating back into my imagination. Clearly, my sister Barb had taught me many life lessons here in this house. As I thought about my encounter with the sink and my "ah ha" moment about sorrow, anger, grief, dying, and surviving, I knew Barb had taught me about death as well. Death didn't have to be the clog in the drain that stopped the water from flowing. I knew how to handle it. It was just part of the journey. It was part of life.

Thanks, Barb. I thought to myself as I turned the key to lock the door. *Thanks #?!* sink.*

301

Chapter 35
The Shirt Off Her Back

When June arrived, I was determined to return to Iowa to participate in the Relay for Life. I had put it off long enough, so come "hell or high water" (one of Barb's favorite sayings), I was going to be there.

Barb's son Robb, his wife Patty and their children and significant others had worked tirelessly on organizing Barb's possessions and cleaning her house. Their efforts were a true labor of love. True to Barb's character, they tried to carry on her spirit of generosity. They sold items and donated the money to the American Cancer Society, but their greatest achievement, their greatest brainstorm, was making Barb's Relay for Life shirts into quilt blocks. Two quilts consisting of twenty blocks each were created from the shirts. It was overwhelming to think Barb had participated in that many Relay for Life fundraisers.

Robb and his family had decided to sell raffle tickets for the quilts, announcing the winners at the Relay for Life walk, and donating the money raised to the American Cancer Society. Barb would have loved this idea. What a symbolic gesture it was as well. Truly in the end, Barb gave the very shirts off of her back to raise money in order to fund finding a cure for cancer. Even after her death, her family had found a way for Barb the Warrior Chick to be victorious over the disease she had battled for so many years.

Mary and I, the two partners in crime, arrived at the Relay for Life together. We followed the signs to the registration area and picked up our shirts. I explained mine was one color to signify I was a cancer survivor, and hers was a different color to signify she was a participant in the activities. While I hadn't taken part in the Relay for Life in Iowa for several years, I had participated in a couple back in

Colorado. I wasn't the expert Barb was, but I was proud of myself for knowing some of the ropes.

Mary and I ducked into the nearest bathroom to put on our relay shirts, giggling as we lamented the fact that we no longer had girlish figures. We stuffed our regular shirts into our purses and headed out to explore the surrounding area.

As we circulated through the booths, which were selling a variety of items to raise money for the cause, we quickly realized our identities had changed from Mary and Pam to Barb's sisters. Barb was an icon to this group. Our chests puffed up with pride, not enough to regain our girlish figures from the cruel grips of gravity and aging, but enough to show others we were proud of our sister.

We followed the sound of familiar laughter to the booth where our family members were located. I caught my breath as I saw the quilts for the first time. They were beautiful, absolutely beautiful! Each t-shirt square was a different color creating a cheerful rainbow effect. The background of one quilt was royal blue and the other was a deep purple. One of Barb's bowling buddies had volunteered to do the quilting as a tribute to our beloved sister. The craftsmanship and attention to detail was exquisite. Clearly, the quilts were a labor of love. The marketing for the quilt raffle tickets had been phenomenal. Ads had appeared in the local papers and on Facebook. Local businesses had also helped to spread the word about this special fundraiser. Hundreds of dollars of raffle tickets had already been sold. Today would be the last day of sales, then the drawing would be held, and the quilts would have new forever homes.

Our family members hung out at the booth for most of the morning, selling a few more raffle tickets, enjoying each other's company, and eventually eating lunch.

When the time for the survivors' lap arrived, I was nervous. I had promised myself I would participate in the lap as a tribute to Barb. The location for this Relay for Life was at the county courthouse, which was in a town just a few miles from our hometown. Relay teams continuously walked on the sidewalks, which encircled the courthouse. Money was donated to the teams for the amount of time or the number of laps each team completed. During the survivors' lap, teams usually took a break from walking in order to free up the course, but also to honor the survivors.

My heart was pounding rapidly as I joined the other survivors at the start line. As I viewed the people of all ages, shapes, colors, and sizes gathering in their purple survivor shirts, I realized once again that cancer doesn't discriminate. Everyone is fair game. Although I didn't know a single person in the group, I felt we had something in common. Obviously, we had survived cancer, and that fact created a bond, a friendship, and a kinship between us.

The "race" began, and I felt confident as the purple mob rounded the first turn. Then it happened. I saw the quilts on display in our family's booth. The vibrant colors were not to be ignored or denied, and reminded me of my promise to Barb that one day we would walk this course not as sisters but as survivors. I felt surges of guilt pulse through my mind, knowing my promise could never become a reality. There was always a class to take, a reunion to attend, or a wedding to celebrate instead. Now because of my unkept promise, I was walking the course alone, and Barb was gone forever. I glanced at the quilts one more time, and began to cry. My pace slowed until I was standing still. The other survivors continued, nonchalantly passing me. Suddenly, I felt an arm around my waist.

"You can do this! I'm right here beside you."

Was it Barb? You can do this. That is what Barb had told me throughout my cancer journey, throughout my entire life. I had heard those words of wisdom from her so many times. You can do this!

I gathered enough courage to glance beside me. There was my partner in crime, my beloved Mary.

"Kick it in high gear, girl, or we are going to lose this race," she taunted me. "I don't care what color of shirt I have on, I'm going to walk with you!"

"I wouldn't have it any other way," I told her as I slipped my arm over her shoulder. "I always told Barb that we would walk the survivors' lap together, and I never made good on that promise," I confessed to Mary.

"She is here with us now. You know that don't you?" Mary asked.

"I know," I answered.

"Consider your promise complete," Mary assured me.

"You know Barb always spoiled me from the day I was born," I told Mary. "Who is going to spoil me now?"

"I'll do it," Mary quickly replied.

"Are you sure?" I questioned with a hopeful tone in my voice. "You don't even know what is involved."

"I don't care. I'll do it anyway," she said curtly.

"It's really not that complicated. You send me a card on my birthday. You send me gifts periodically for no apparent reason. I stay at your house when I come home to visit, and we tell each other we love one another whenever we are together or talk on the phone," I explained.

Mary looked at me and laughed. "I already do all of those things, you goof."

"Yeah, you do, and I love you for it," I told her. "I guess I turned out pretty good considering I am a 'spoiled little brat.'"

"Yeah, you turned out pretty good," Mary laughed. "Now quit talking and walk. Barb wouldn't want us to come in last place."

Mary and Pam at The Relay For Life

307

Chapter 36
Cancer Changes Everything

I was sitting at the dining room table with the blank screen of my laptop staring at me as if taunting me to press the keys to write a story. I was working on a collection of short essays titled <u>A Christmas to Remember.</u> I had decided to write about the Christmas Greg had given me a trip to anywhere in the world as a celebration of completing my radiation treatments. As the words began to fill the screen, I quickly realized this was more than just a short story. It was a book.

My heart pounded rapidly in my chest, not from excitement or anticipation, but from fear. I knew exactly what God was calling me to do. He wanted me to write about my experiences with cancer, not only as a patient, but also as a loved one of someone who had been diagnosed. He wanted me to share the ups, downs, twists, turns, and detours with the hope that my testimony could help others on their journeys. I could feel the familiar element of self-doubt overtaking my sense of logic and squelching all other emotions.

Would anyone even care about my journey? Was my story only relevant to me? What if I poured my heart out only to be criticized and scorned? Was I strong enough to withstand that?

Just as the stones I had thrown into the lake during my childhood created ripples from the energy of the rocks displacing the water, God was calling me to create ripples in other people's lives through the energy of my story. God was on my side so what more could I ask for? He wouldn't forsake me but would only love and empower me.

I could clearly hear and feel God calling me to complete the task at hand, to do His will, to write the book. But I was still afraid. I was afraid of failure. I was afraid of rejection. I wanted desperately to plug my ears and chant, "La, la, la" so I could no longer hear His call. But that would be childish. Besides, the voice I was hearing wasn't from an external force. It was coming from deep within me. It wasn't the deep male voice of God that movies portray. It was a female voice. It was Barb whispering over and over, "You can do this. You can do this."

As a last ditch effort to turn off the voice and to redirect my attention, I plugged my headphones into the side of my laptop and placed them over my ears. A quick click on my favorite playlist resulted in a beloved lyric filling my head . . . "Here I Am," performed by Rebecca Saint James. I closed my eyes in order to concentrate on the words, which soon became my prayer. Just as the lyrics of the song implied, God was asking for people He could send to do His work, to complete His will. I felt I had answered this call. I had given my life to God. I had devoted my life to believing in Him, making Him my hope, serving Him by serving others, and by ultimately loving Him. The song so eloquently summed up my life. *Here I am, Lord. I surrender my life to You to do with it as You will. Here I am.*

As the music faded, I removed my headphones and placed my head face down on the tabletop to think. My husband passed by the dining room, stopping momentarily he asked, "Are you okay?"

"Yep, I'm good," I replied keeping my head on the tabletop with my eyes closed. "I'm just thinking."

Being the wise man he is, he continued on his way leaving me alone with my thoughts.

Since I was a small child, I had prayed each morning for God to give me the strength to do His will. As an adult woman, this prayer had morphed into a more sophisticated form of words that I printed on a white sheet of copy paper, and I displayed on the side of the metal filing cabinet in every classroom I ever inhabited. These words became a reminder of my life's purpose, "To meet the needs of many by serving One." I truly felt if I put my service to God first, everything else would fall into place.

This challenge to write a book about my cancer journey was just one more example of God fulfilling my life long request to have strength to do His will, but I had a free will. I could make the choice to share my story according to His plan, or I could take the safe route and keep my journey to myself.

As images of my cancer journey flashed through my imagination, I realized how cancer had changed every aspect of my life. The diagnosis had given me a new, positive, grateful outlook on life. The surgery had transformed my body. I had been forced to give up a few relationships, but I had also gained many new friends. My finances had been drained, replenished, and drained again. My new outlook on life created a domino effect of prioritizing what was truly important and what was a waste of precious time. This led to letting go of my teaching career in order to search for a career I loved. My career change led to a new environment, a new home, a new identity and self-image. I learned lessons on how to live life to the fullest and lessons from Steve, Dad, and Barb on how to die with grace, dignity, hope, and purpose.

I thought of the words Barb had spoken to me that created a huge change in my daily perspective. "It's not about you," she had told me. When I stopped thinking about myself in order to put others first, my entire life changed. That's when the ripples from the rock thrown into the water had enough power and energy to reach the shore, to not only change my life but the lives of the people around me.

I thought about when I had invited, not only the students in my classroom to join me on my cancer journey, but the entire school community as well. At the time, I didn't realize their lives would be changed forever.

Through our journey together, we had learned how to conquer our fear of cancer by having open, honest conversations. We had learned that through our actions, we could become victors over cancer rather than victims of cancer. We had learned about the power of teamwork, realizing by working together we could accomplish so much more than what we could individually. We had learned about the power of empathy and generosity. These characteristics helped each individual to grow, mature, and come closer becoming the best possible person he or she could be.

Even though what we learned could never be found in one of our textbooks, curriculum guides, or on a standardized test, I believed all of these lessons were not only relevant but life changing.

I had gone on a physical journey halfway around the world on a quest to find meaning in my life. Fortunately, after a weeklong process, I found it. Life is about people, the emotions we share, the relationships we construct. It is about the relationships we build with each other and the relationship we build with God. I learned we are unique masterpieces created by God. How we live, how we handle the challenges life throws at us, and how we view death and grief are also as unique as each individual. These differences need to be acknowledged, respected, and even admired.

Some people may believe life is a series of spontaneous events, but not in my book, and I mean that both figuratively and literally. God has a plan for each of us. But we must remember that we also have a free will and can say yes or no to His plan. By following His plan, by saying yes to God's challenges for me, my relationship with Him had grown. The depth of that relationship has known no boundaries. Perhaps that was the greatest change of all. Yes, it was true. Cancer changes everything . . . if you let it.

I raised my head from the tabletop and placed my headphones on my ears. I clicked on the song "Here I Am" from my playlist. As the words of

Rebecca Saint James echoed through the
headphones and into my heart, I began to write. .

Ah, Billy Joel's Greatest Hits. I
removed the disk from the CD
holder attached to the visor
on the passenger side of my car. I
kissed the CD knowing that would
be the closest I would ever come
to kissing Billy Joel. Then I
quickly popped the disk into the
player . . .

Sources of Information

https://en.wikipedia.org/wiki/Blois
https://en.wikipedia.org/wiki/Chateau_d_A
mboise
https://en.wikipedia.org/wiki/Chateau_de_C
henonceau
https://en.wikipedia.org/wiki/Claude_Monet
https://en.wikipedia.org/wiki/Deauville
https://en.wikipedia.org/wiki/Gold_Beach
https://en.wikipedia.org/wiki/History_of_the
_Palace_of_Versailles
https://en.wikipedia.org/wiki/Honfleur
https://en.wikipedia.org/wiki/Invasion_of_N
ormandy
https://en.wikipedia.org/wiki/Leonardo_da_
Vinci
https://en.wikipedia.org/wiki/Louvre
https://en.wikipedia.org/wiki/Mont_Saint_M
ichel
https://en.wikipedia.org/wiki/Rennes
https://en.wikipedia.org/wiki/Rouen_Cathed
ral
https://en.wikipedia.org/wiki/Saint_Malo
https://en.wikipedia.org/wiki/Waldo_Canyo
n_fire

Books
by Pam Pottorff

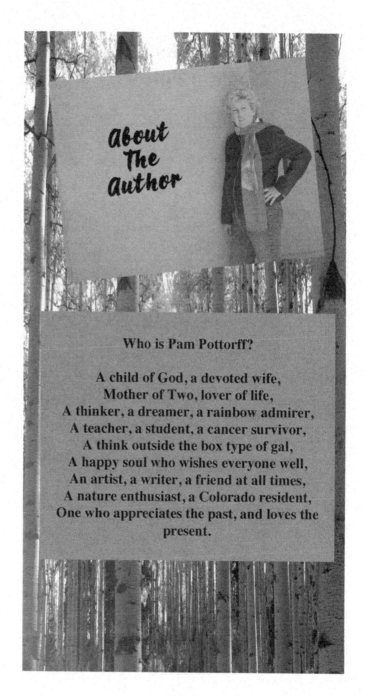

about
The
author

Who is Pam Pottorff?

A child of God, a devoted wife,
Mother of Two, lover of life,
A thinker, a dreamer, a rainbow admirer,
A teacher, a student, a cancer survivor,
A think outside the box type of gal,
A happy soul who wishes everyone well,
An artist, a writer, a friend at all times,
A nature enthusiast, a Colorado resident,
One who appreciates the past, and loves the
present.